SENIORS
GUIDE
SERIES

Table of Contents

Introduction

Apple's next-generation System on a Chip (SoC) for Macs is the M2. It signifies Apple's continued efforts to move away from the Intel chips used in Macs until 2020.

Before the introduction of Apple silicon, Macs utilized multiple chips for CPU, I/O, and security. However, Apple's efforts to integrate these chips have made the M2 significantly faster and more efficient than Intel chips. Apple's unified memory architecture is also notable, enabling all M2 technologies to access the same data without switching between multiple memory pools.

For less intensive tasks that do not require as much power, such as web browsing, four high-efficiency cores consume one-tenth as much power to preserve battery life.

Apple claims that the M2 chip is constructed using the 5-nanometer technology of the next generation, which provides improved performance per watt. It employs 20 billion transistors, 25 percent more than the M1 and adds 100GB/s to the memory bandwidth.

The M2 chip is 1.4 times faster than the M1 chip, with a CPU 18 percent faster, a GPU 35 percent more powerful, and a Neural Engine 40 percent faster.

In terms of multicore performance, Geekbench benchmarks have confirmed that the M2 chip is up to 20 percent faster than the M1 chip.

The single-core score of the M2, which runs at 3.49GHz compared to the M1's 3.2GHz, is 1919, which is around 12 percent quicker than the M1's single-core score of 1707. The M2 achieved a multi-core score of 8928, approximately 20 percent higher than the M1's score of 7419.

Regarding the Metal benchmark, the M2 chip scored 30627, significantly improving over the M1's score of 21001. The M2 chip provides up to a 10-core GPU instead of the M1 chip's maximum of 8 cores.

On top of being faster than most Intel chips, Apple's silicon chips are incredibly battery-efficient. With the M2 chip, the MacBook Air's battery lasts up to 18 hours, while the 13-inch MacBook Pro's battery lasts up to 20 hours.

Despite its incredible speed improvements, the M1 chip is more battery-efficient than any other Mac chip Apple has released to date.

The M1 Mac's battery life is up to twice as long as that of previous-generation Macs. The 13-inch MacBook Pro has the longest battery life of any Mac, lasting up to 20 hours. That is twice the battery life of the previous model.

The book has been prepared for beginners and seniors with top-level tips and tricks to help users of the MacBook master and operate the laptop like experts.

This guide has covered you if you're switching from Windows computers and other devices to the MacBook for the first time.

Chapter 1:

Terminology

1. USB (Universal Serial Bus): USB (Universal Serial Bus) is a data transmission protocol that enables the exchange of data between devices and their peripherals. There are USB ports in computers, keyboards and trackpads, digital cameras and camcorders, printers and other devices that can be connected to a computer. Nearly every other device that can be linked to a computer also has a USB port. For instance, a keyboard, a mouse, a trackpad, a printer, and other devices that can be connected to a computer all have USB connections. Devices that don't need a lot of power can also be powered by USB.

This cable features a standard USB connector on one end and a Micro-USB connector on the other.

There have been three major USB specifications have been implemented: USB 1.1, USB 2.0, and USB 3.0. The primary distinction between them is in terms of speed. USB 2.0 and 3.0 are speedier than their predecessors. Because USB is backward-compatible, you can connect a device designed for USB 2.0 to another device equipped with USB 3.0 ports.

There are three different types of USB connectors: the traditional rectangular one used On Macs; the trapezoid-shaped mini-connector seen on some digital cameras and hard drives; and the minuscule Micro-USB connector found on modern Kindle readers and other electronic devices.

2. FireWire: FireWire (also known as IEEE 1394) is a technology that allows for connecting devices that are compatible with it to work together. The technology was developed for applications requiring quick data transfer, such as computers, storage devices, audio interfaces, and video equipment's like camcorders and video interfaces.

Although faster FireWire standards exist, the most common connectors are FireWire 400 and FireWire 800. FireWire 800, the most recent standard, allows for much quicker data transfer rates than FireWire 400, which was the previous standard. FireWire 800 is backward compatible with devices that use FireWire 400 as their interface standard. Each one has a unique connection. The FireWire 400 connector is oblong, with one end rounded and the other flat, and most computers use it. The form of the FireWire 800 connection is rectangular. Micro FireWire connectors are also available as an optional accessory. These connectors are compact and have a trapezoidal form. Recent Macs equipped with a FireWire port support FireWire 800.

3. Lightning connector: This is the proprietary connector used in the most recent iPod touch, iPhone, iPad, and iPad mini versions, among other devices. It takes the place of the 30-pin dock connector used on prior generations of iOS devices and iPods, among other things. Comparatively speaking, the Lightning connector functions regardless of the side facing up. The USB connector on the other end of the cable, like the 30-pin connector on the other end of the cable that precedes it, allows data and power to be transferred to an associated device.

4. Thunderbolt: Thunderbolt is the data transfer protocol of the twenty-first century. It differs from FireWire or USB because it allows for simultaneous data and video communications. In this case, you could connect your Mac to a display like Apple's Thunderbolt Display with a single Thunderbolt cable. The video from your Mac would show up on display, and you could connect other devices to your Mac through the USB, FireWire, Thunderbolt, and Ethernet ports on the back of the display.

Thunderbolt offers up to 20 times the performance of USB 2.0 and up to 12 times the performance of the former compared to the latter. A single Thunderbolt port can accommodate up to six compatible devices simultaneously. With the use of an appropriate adaptor, you may connect USB, FireWire, and gigabit ethernet devices to a Thunderbolt port. There are Thunderbolt ports available on the following Mac models:

- Apple MacBook Pro
- Apple MacBook Pro
- MacBook Pro
- MacBook Air
- Mac mini Server
- Mac mini
- iMac

5. Mini DisplayPort: Mini DisplayPort offers only digital video and resolutions up to 2560 by 1600. The connector is a small rectangle with two rounded corners, like a Thunderbolt connector. It can be used in a Thunderbolt port. Mini DisplayPort to VGA, DVI, or HDMI adapters are available.

6. DVI (Digital Visual Interface): The DVI connector can be used as both analog and digital. It supports resolutions up to 2560 by 1600 pixels and comes in three connector types: DVI, Mini-DVI, and Micro-DVI. Two blocks of straight round pins next to a larger thin rectangular pin identify these rectangular connections. Apple used DVI connectors until 2008, when Mini Display Port connectors were introduced.

7. HDMI (High-Definition Multimedia Interface): Modern HDTVs and AV receivers have HDMI ports. They're on today's retina MacBook Pros and Mac minis and will be on Apple's next Mac Pro in the fall of 2013. HDMI supports resolutions up to 2560 x 1600 pixels at 75 fps and 4096 x 2160 pixels at 24 fps. HDMI supports audio and video.

8. VGA: Video Graphics Array (VGA) is a huge 15-pin trapezoidal connection found on old computers and cheap video cards. Some modern televisions and computer monitors still have these connectors. VGA delivers up to 2048 by 1536 pixels. Although Macs haven't had VGA ports for a long time, you may connect them to a VGA monitor, TV, or projector with an adaptor.

Networking, both wired and wireless

Some call the ability to wirelessly connect your computer and mobile devices to the Internet "magic." These additional — and more exact — procedures and methods include.

9. Ethernet: Ethernet is a type of wired computer networking (that is, in networked devices that are located in the same physical space and share a common router address). As with a telephone plug, an Ethernet connection fits into its host socket like a piece of wire. In terms of Ethernet, there are three types: 10Base-T, 100Base-T, or 1000Base-T. (also known as gigabit ethernet). Their speed varies a lot. If you use 10Base-T or 100Base-T or 1000Base-T, you can only send and receive 10Mbps (or one gigabit per second).

Ethernet connections can be much faster than Wi-Fi connections, depending on the devices used to connect to them. You can use your Mac if it has gigabit Ethernet, but your connected device only has 100Base-T. Therefore, your Mac will have to send data at a slower speed. A lot of people use Ethernet, which has a lot of space. An Ethernet cable can be used when there is no Wi-Fi service in your area.

10. WIFI: Wi-Fi refers to any IEEE 802.11 compliant wireless local area network. What exactly does this mean? If they support the standard, they can share data and communicate. Depending on the circumstances, data may need to be exchanged between devices linked to the same local network or wirelessly to the Internet.

Wireless standards of the eighth generation (802.11a) and b (802.11) are available. With each final letter of the alphabet, the speed gradually increases (as does range, in some cases). Ethernet connections are more secure than Wi-Fi connections. To steal data from an Ethernet network, an attacker must physically tap into the network; to take data from a Wi-Fi network, an intruder must be adjacent to the network (possessing the necessary tools for intercepting and decrypting data).

The AirPort uses Apple's Wi-Fi technology. Turning off AirPort refers to your Mac's Wi-Fi, which is what most users mean.

11. Bluetooth: Bluetooth is a wireless data transfer method with a shorter range than Wi-Fi (approximately 30 feet). Bluetooth allows some portable devices and keyboards to connect to a Mac.

12. Bonjour: Bonjour is Apple's networking solution that requires no configuration. It is a sophisticated combination of technologies to make local networking easier. Anyone who has set up a wireless printer and then launched Mac OS X understands how convenient it is to have your computer quickly connect to the printer without performing a series of time-consuming chores.

13. 3G & 4G: 3G & 4G (G stands for generation) are data-carrying wireless technologies used by cellular networks. It is not always the case that 4G speeds outperform 3G.

For starters, 4G comes in various flavors, including HSPA+, WiMAX, and LTE. Furthermore, just because a network is 4G does not imply that it is faster than a fast 3G network. An iOS update, for example, updated the menu bar of certain iPhone models from 3G to 4G. AT&T branded its HSPA+ network as 4G even though it provided no speed enhancement.

Hardware for networks

Even though it may be enough to call the thing that makes your wireless network work "that blinking box over there," there may come a time when you need to know what that box is called and what it seems to be doing. For example, when you're on the phone with your ISP's support team.

1. broadband modem: A broadband modem is a type of computer hardware. It connects to the cable that runs through your wall and your computer at home or work. The connection will be created over a phone line if you have a DSL connection. You should understand that if you have a cable connection, it will be just that: a cable connection. If you have a fiber-based system, you will also need to add another cable to your system. You can connect the box to the Internet since you have an Internet Service Provider. You cannot connect to the Internet if your Wi-Fi is turned off. A customer service representative may request that you "reset your modem" by unplugging it from the wall outlet. It would be best to look for this box near the top of your list of things to find.

A broadband modem typically contains numerous lights, some of which blink. Each features a power indicator, a status indicator, and a LAN indicator (local area network). Ensure you understand what these lights mean when your connection is working properly. Something is awry when the green light turns red.

2. Router: A router is required as a traffic cop for your home network. Your router must ensure that the correct data is delivered to and from your Mac, iPhone or iPad, Apple TV, or smart TV. Typically, it accomplishes this by assigning a unique address to each device. Routers, both wireless and wired, are available for purchase. Wireless routers, such as AirPort Base Stations, are available in stores.

You should do this if your cable operator has provided you with a modem/router combination box. This box includes a single ethernet port connecting your Mac to a network. However, you also wish to connect an Apple TV and a smart TV to the ethernet. It is your responsibility to keep things running smoothly.

The network switch you purchase is important (in this case, an ethernet switch). Furthermore, the switch serves as a traffic cop. When a router transmits data to a specific address, such as your Apple TV's address, the data is delivered only to the Apple TV and not to the rest of your network's infrastructure. An Ethernet hub, which is becoming less prevalent, performs the same function but does not route traffic. All information submitted to the hub's input is distributed to all devices that are connected to the hub. As a result, data transmission takes longer and there is a greater likelihood of data collisions.

Switches can have up to a million ports and a wide range of speeds. Most of today's switches can handle connection speeds of 10/100/1000 megabits per second. An integrated switch manages three LAN ports on Apple's AirPort Extreme Base Station. The portable base station contains three ports.

Chapter 2:

Setting Up

2.1 MacBook Air Hardware and Keyboard

Design:

In 2022, Apple completely redesigned the MacBook Air, the first significant redesign of the range since 2010. In place of the MacBook Air's long-standing tapered chassis, the upgraded model has a flat, MacBook Pro-style body that is the same thickness from front to back.

The redesigned MacBook Air is roughly the same size as the previous generation, but there are a few minor variations. Its thickness of 11.3mm is considerably less than the thickest point of the previous model (16.1mm). Its dimensions are 11.97 inches long by 8.46 inches deep, and its weight of 2.7 pounds is slightly less than that of the 2.8-pound model from the previous generation.

On the left side are two Thunderbolt/USB-C connections, as well as a MagSafe charging port and a 3.5mm headphone jack. Another design feature borrowed from the MacBook Pro is Apple's addition of four feet.

Similar to the model from the previous generation, it has black bezels around the screen, a black Magic keyboard without a Touch Bar, and a sizable Force Touch trackpad. It is simply a more compact and lightweight MacBook Pro.

In addition to Silver, the MacBook Air is also offered in Space Gray, Starlight (a light gold), and Midnight, a brand-new deep blue hue.

Keyboard and Trackpad:

The Magic Keyboard from the MacBook Air's predecessor is still in use. Unlike Apple's butterfly keyboards in earlier Macs, it has a scissor-switch mechanism that can withstand dust and other contaminants without malfunctioning.

The keyboard on the MacBook Air has a scissor mechanism that provides 1 mm of key travel, a steady key feel, and a rubber dome created by Apple that can store more potential energy for a key push that is more responsive. The keyboard also has backlit keys controlled by an ambient light sensor to light up the keys in dark places.

The MacBook Air lacks a Touch Bar and includes a complete row of function keys, just like the M1 Pro and M1 Max MacBook Pro models.

A sizable Force Touch trackpad is located underneath the keyboard and is the same as in previous iterations. Users of the Force Touch trackpad can press anywhere on the trackpad to receive the same reaction because it lacks conventional buttons and is powered by a collection of Force Sensors. Users receive tactile sensation when using the trackpad in place of the actual button press, thanks to a taptic engine powered by magnets.

The Force Touch trackpad enables both a light push, which serves as a standard click, and a deeper press, or "force click," which functions as a different motion and, among other things, displays definitions for a highlighted word.

Touch ID:

The Touch ID fingerprint sensor on the M2 MacBook Air is situated next to the function keys at the top of the keyboard. Your fingerprint data and private information are safe with Touch ID, thanks to a Secure Enclave.

When a finger is placed on the sensor, Touch ID on the MacBook Air unlocks the computer without needing a password. It may also be used to make Apple Pay transactions in Safari and takes the place of passwords for password-protected apps.

Ports:

Additionally, the MacBook Air has a new MagSafe 3 charging port that is the same as the charging port added to the 14- and 16-inch MacBook Pro models. The MacBook Air has two Thunderbolt 3/USB-C ports that support transfer speeds of up to 40Gb/s.

High-impedance headphones can be used with the 3.5mm headphone jack.

Display:

Due to thinner side bezels, Apple raised the size of the display on the 2022 MacBook Air, which now measures 13.6 inches. Although it resembles the Retina display from the previous generation, Apple calls the display on the MacBook Air a Liquid Retina display.

Like the MacBook Pro, the MacBook Air sports a notch to provide access to a 1080p webcam while providing additional display space.

The MacBook Air has a resolution of 2560 x 1664, 224 pixels per inch, and 1 billion color support. Its brightness is 500 nits, compared to 400 nits in the model from the previous generation. For vibrant, true-to-life colors, it supports P3 Wide color.

The MacBook Air's display uses True Tone, a technology that adjusts color to match ambient illumination better. The MacBook Air models come with a multi-channel ambient light sensor to power True Tone and measure the room's brightness and color temperature.

The MacBook Air can adapt the display's color and brightness to match the lighting in the room after determining the white balance, providing a more realistic viewing experience that reduces eyestrain.

M2 Apple Silicon Chip:

The M2, which Apple incorporated into the MacBook Air, was the M1's replacement and the company's first silicon chip, which was released in November 2020. The M2 has an 8-core CPU, just like the M1, but it supports nine or ten GPU cores, increasing from the seven or eight cores supported by the model from the previous generation.

Apple claims that the M2 processor has improved performance per watt and is constructed using cutting-edge 5-nanometer technology. It has 20 billion transistors, 25% more than the M1 and adds 100 GB/s of additional memory bandwidth.

The M2 chip outperforms the M1 by 1.4 times and the older MacBook Air models that were Intel-based by 15 times. The CPU is 18% faster, the GPU is 35% more potent, and the RAM is 40% bigger.

The M2, which runs at 3.49 GHz compared to 3.2GHz for the M1, has a single-core score of 1919, which is around 12 % faster than the M1 MacBook Air's single-core score of 1707. The multi-core score for the M2 was 8928, up roughly 20% from the M1 model's score of 7419.

In terms of the Metal test, the M2 chip scored 30627, a significant increase from the M1 chip's score of 21001. The highest GPU core count of the M2 processor is 10, compared to the M1's 8 cores.

Like the M1 MacBook Air, the M2 MacBook Air doesn't have fans and can run quietly.

Memory and Storage:

Up to 24GB of Unified Memory and up to 2TB of SSD storage are supported by the M2 MacBook Air. The base model comes with 256GB of storage and 8GB of memory.

Battery life:

The Apple TV app to view movies on the M2 MacBook Air can extend battery life by up to 18 hours, while wireless web browsing can extend battery life by up to 15 hours.

A 30W USB-C power adapter is included with the base model, while a 35W Dual USB-C Port Compact Power Adapter is included with the base model with the 10-core GPU. With a 67W USB-C Power Adapter, the MacBook Air can be fast-charged and charged via MagSafe.

Other Features:

Connectivity:

The standard Wi-Fi 802.11ax, often known as Wi-Fi 6, is supported by the MacBook Air and is faster and more effective than 802.11ac WiFi. As well, Bluetooth 5.0 is supported.

Speakers and Microphone:

Two tweeters and two ultrathin woofers in the four-speaker sound system Apple installed on the MacBook Air improve stereo separation and vocal quality.

Additionally, the MacBook Air supports spatial audio and wide stereo. The built-in speakers can play music or videos with Dolby Atmos and offer spatial audio. The third generation of AirPods, AirPods Pro, and AirPods Max also offers spatial audio with dynamic head tracking.

The MacBook Air also has a three-microphone array with directional beamforming for improved sound clarity on video conversations.

FaceTime Camera:

The same 1080p FaceTime HD camera as the MacBook Air is included in the 2021 14- and 16-inch MacBook Pro models. According to Apple, it is powered by an upgraded image signal processor with the computational video that improves video quality and has double the resolution and low-light capabilities of the previous model.

2.2 MacBook Pro Hardware and Keyboard

Display:

The 2022 MacBook Pro with M2 Chip features a 13-inch Retina display with 2560 x 1600 resolution at 227 pixels per inch (PPI), True Tome technology, P3 Wide color support, and 500 nits of brightness.

True Tone technology uses a multi-channel ambient light sensor to adjust the display to the brightness of the environment to reduce eye strain when using the MacBook.

The P3 Wide Color has a wider color gamut than the standard RGB displays, so the colors appear more vibrant and natural.

Design:

The new MacBook Pro offers an identical design to its predecessor, with a rectangular shape, an aluminum chassis, and slender bezels surrounding the display. The MacBook Pro offers two color options: silver and space gray.

The M2 MacBook Pro comes with a slender hinge, a 3.5mm headphone jack, a big trackpad, a Touch Bar, two Thunderbolt ports, speaker grilles on the side, and the Apple logo at the back. The MacBook Pro has a thickness of 14.9 millimeters, a length of 11.97 inches, and a width of 8.36 inches. It is about 0.13 kg heavier than the MacBook Air. It has an active cooling process that keeps the laptop cooler for better performance.

Apple has decided to ditch the butterfly mechanism for its keyboard and has integrated the revamped Magic Keyboard that was initially used in the 16-inch MacBook Pro.

It comes with backlit keys that are controlled by an ambient light sensor to make the keys illuminate in a dark environment.

Processor:

The M2 Chip replaces the M1 processor that was first featured in November 2020. The new processor is 1.4 times faster than its predecessor. It offers a 35% more powerful GPU, an 18% more efficient CPU, and a 40% faster Neural Engine than its predecessor. The processor runs at 3.49GHz. It integrates a 5-nanometer architecture and comes with an eight-core CPU and nine or ten GPU cores. It is made up of twenty billion transistors. The battery life has also been improved. It features a 58.2 WHr battery.

Touch Bar & Touch ID:

Apple has decided to bring back the Touch Bar to the 13-inch M2 MacBook Pro. Built into the keyboard, the Touch Bar is an OLED retina multi-touch display that replaces the function buttons. You can perform gestures such as swiping, tapping, or sliding and depending on what software is being used on the Mac; it can do a wide range of things.

The Touch Bar is positioned on the same horizontal plane as the keyboards. It features a matte-style display that fits perfectly with the buttons on the keyboard. It offers True Tone, which allows the white balance to be adjustable and match the room's lighting conditions. Next to the Touch Bar is the Touch ID fingerprint sensor. It can confirm purchases made with Apple Pay, unlock the Mac, or open apps without a password.

Trackpad

Apple has integrated a large Force Touch trackpad on the new MacBook Pro. It doesn't feature traditional buttons but is driven by a series of Force Sensors that support multi-touch. It allows pressing on the trackpad to deliver the same feedback.

The trackpad provides haptic feedback when using it. It replaces the sensation that comes with pressing the physical keys. It offers light pressing and force-click; these gestures offer different functions. You can force-click to see details about a file, add events to the calendar, add a pin to a location, and more.

Connectivity/Ports:

It has two Thunderbolt 4/USB-C ports and can be utilized for charging. It also supports fast charging. The Thunderbolt 3 transfer speed can reach up to 40 Gb/s, while the USB transfer speed can reach up to 10 Gb/s.

It supports Wi-Fi 6 and Bluetooth 5.0.

Memory & Storage:

The base model incorporates 8GB of RAM and 256GB of storage. It can also support up to 24GB of unified memory and 2TB of SSD.

FaceTime camera & microphones:

The front camera has not changed, although the processor allows for a vivid and more precise picture. Apple has added the same 720p HD camera to facilitate FaceTime calls. Apple has also added studio-quality mics for improved sound.

2.3 MacBook Pro Vs MacBook Air

Here, we will present comparisons of the MacBook Pro and MacBook Air.

Differences between the MacBook Pro and MacBook Air include:

- The MacBook Air has a slim, wedge-style, while the MacBook Pro has a thicker, slab-like design.
- MacBook Air comes in space gray, silver, midnight, and starlight. The MacBook Pro is available in silver and space gray.
- MacBook Airs weighs 2.7 pounds, while MacBook Pros weigh 3.5 pounds.
- MacBook Air and MacBook Pro both reach a brightness of up to 500 nits.
- The battery life of the MacBook Air extends up to 18 hours, while that of the MacBook Pro reaches 20 hours.
- MacBook Air has a passive cooling system compared to the passive one found on the MacBook Pro.

- When it comes to stereo speakers, MacBook Air has simple ones. Contrastingly, you will find a high dynamic range of stereo speakers on the MacBook Pro.
- The MacBook Air has a simple three-microphone array with directional beamforming, whereas that of the MacBook Pro is more enhanced since its studio quality.
- MacBook Pro has a touch bar, which is unavailable on the MacBook Air.

2.4 The Very Basics

Setting up a new Mac is straightforward because you only need to follow the on-screen instructions to get off to a good and exciting start. To set up your new Mac:

1. Press the **"power button"** to switch it on.
2. Choose a language that your computer will use across the system, be it English, French, or Spanish; you name it.
3. Click **Continue**, then select the keyboard layout that you prefer.

After selecting the keyboard layout, other things must also be set up. These include network options, location services, Apple ID, and the time zone based on your current location. Depending on the amount of storage that you have on your device, you could also store your iCloud documents on your new Mac. Remember to click **"Enable Siri on this Mac,"** your computer's virtual assistant. Your Mac will then finalize all settings. It is normal to see a spinning wheel and an on-screen message that says "Setting up."

2.5 The Login Screen And Touch ID

It used to be that only Apple iPhones could use Touch ID, but those days are long gone. Until a few years ago, all MacBook Pro and MacBook Air models had a keyboard that could be used with

Touch ID. Setting up Touch ID will only take a few seconds if you're new to Apple. It will make a big difference in your daily life.

2.5.1 What Is Touch ID And How Does It Work?

MacBook Touch ID is the name of Apple's fingerprint identification sensor on the device's keyboard. It's a sort of biometric security designed to be more convenient than putting in a passcode or password, particularly on mobile devices like iPhones and iPads, which we use hundreds of times daily. To register up to five fingerprints on a MacBook Air or MacBook Pro, you must create a separate user account for each fingerprint you want to utilize.

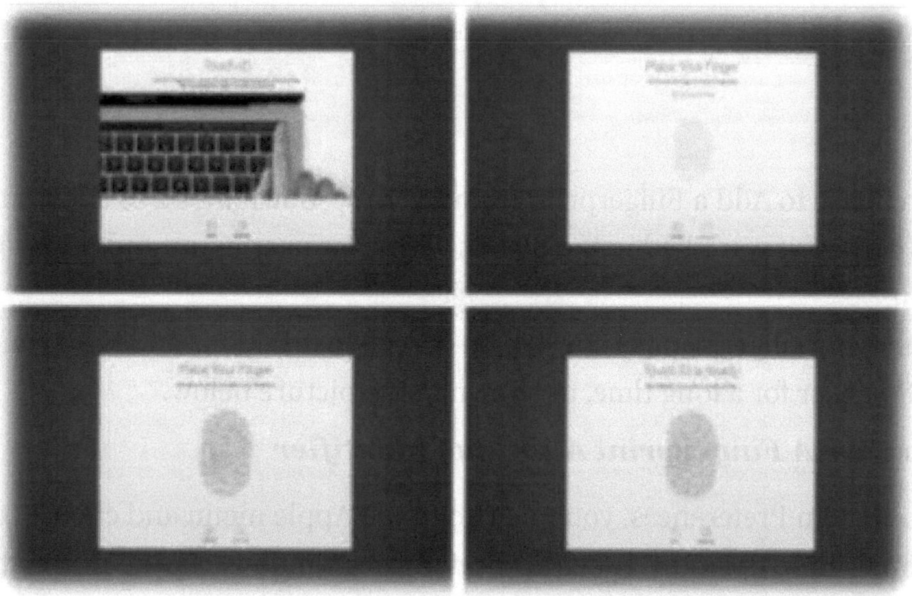

The following actions will be available to you once your fingerprint has been successfully registered on your MacBook Air or MacBook Pro:

- Upon awakening from sleep, go to your user account and log in (you'll be requested to enter your password the first time you log in).
- If each user has their own set of saved fingerprints, you can switch between them from sleep.

2.5.2 How To Configure And Manage The Touch ID Feature On Your Mac.

When you start up your MacBook Air or MacBook Pro for the first time, you'll be asked to set up Touch ID. However, you can always register more fingerprints at any time. For each user account on your Mac, you can keep up to three fingerprints, for a total of five fingerprints across all of them. In the MacBook Air or MacBook Pro, these fingerprints are then encrypted and stored in the Secure Enclave. There, they are safe from anyone who wants to see them.

2.5.3 How To Incorporate A Fingerprint In Your Document

- To get to System Preferences, you must go to the Apple menu and choose it.

When you want to open the Touch ID preferences window, choose it from the menu bar.

- You can choose to Add a Fingerprint from the drop-down menu to add a fingerprint.
- It would be best if you filled in the blanks with your user name and password so that you can log in.
- To register your fingerprint, follow the on-screen instructions and keep your finger on the Touch ID sensor for a long time, as shown in the picture below.

2.5.4 How To Give A Fingerprint A Unique Identifier

- To get to System Preferences, you must go to the Apple menu and choose it.
- When you want to open the Touch ID preferences window, choose it from the menu bar.

- To move through the different fingerprint options, hit the Tab key or click on the name of the fingerprint in the drop-down menu.
- It's possible to change the name of your fingerprint.

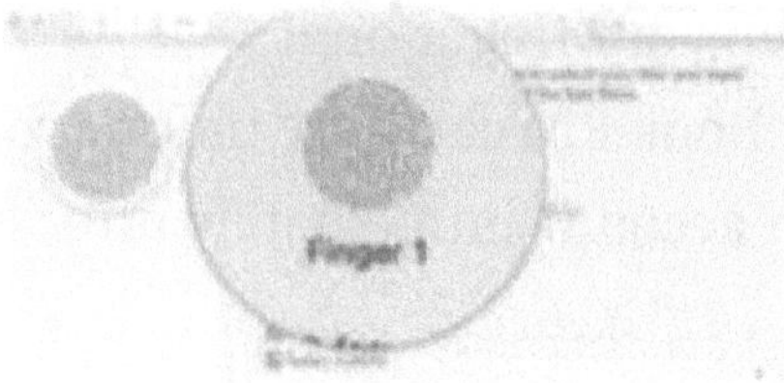

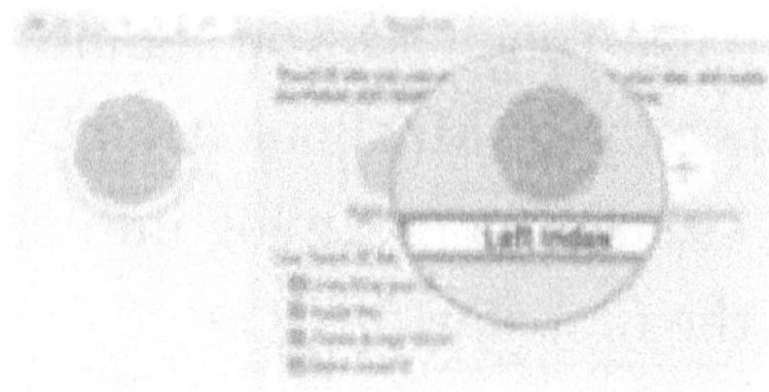

- To go back to the last screen, press the Return key.

2.5.5 How To Permanently Remove A Fingerprint From A Surface

- To get to System Preferences, you must go to the Apple menu and choose it.
- To open the Touch ID preferences window, click on it in the menu bar at the top.
- In the upper left corner of your computer screen, click on the fingerprint icon you want to delete. When you hover your cursor over it, and X will show up.
- This form needs your username and password. Please fill it out with those things.
- To make sure, hit the Delete key.

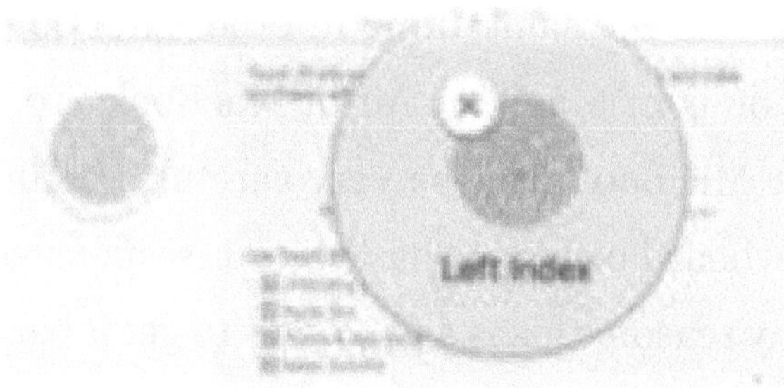

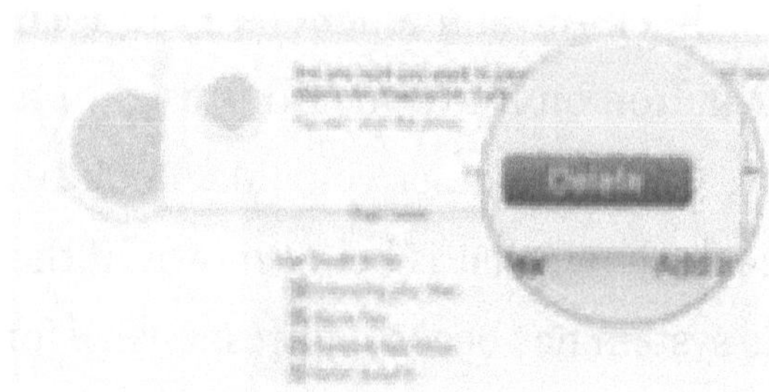

2.5.6 How To Change The Security Settings For Your Touch ID Device

- After you set up your fingerprints, you can say what you want to be able to do with your fingerprints. When you start the game, all three options are checked. You can uncheck any of them by unchecking the box next to the item that you want to uncheck.
- To get to System Preferences, you must go to the Apple menu and choose it.
- To open the Touch ID preferences window, click on it in the menu bar and choose it.
- Choose or choose not to choose the options that you like best.
- Use Touch ID to do the following things:

1. How to Unlock Your Mac
2. Pay with Apple
3. Apple's iTunes and App Store
4. AutoFill in Safari

2.5.7 How To Log In With Touch ID On A Smartphone

- As a first step, if your MacBook Air or MacBook Pro is closed, open it up (or press the Touch ID button).

- If you want to use Touch ID, you should keep your finger on it.
- Multiple users on your MacBook Air or MacBook Pro can have unique fingerprints. Using the Touch ID sensor, you can log into each account immediately after logging in for the first time on the first startup.
- As a first step, if your MacBook Air or MacBook Pro is closed, open it up (or press the Touch ID button).
- Your finger should always stay on the sensor if you want to use Touch ID.
- To buy things from the App Store and iTunes, you can use Touch ID.
- However, even though the MacBook Air and the MacBook Pro with the Touch Bar both have Touch ID authorization for App Store and iTunes purchases, setting it up can be hard. Here's how to set up each app's Touch ID.

2.5.8 Learn How To Conduct A Hard Reset On Your MacBook Air Or MacBook Pro By Following These Steps.

There are some situations where Touch ID can be used instead of the traditional power button on the MacBook Air and MacBook Pro. It can also do the same thing in other situations. The Touch ID button on the keyboard is used to turn on your MacBook Air or MacBook Pro. In the same way, when you reset your MacBook Air or MacBook Pro, be very careful. Useful if the display can't show what is being shown, if the keyboard or cursor has been unresponsive, or if the whole system has become unresponsive for any reason, this is a good way to get it back.

- Keep the Touch ID button pressed and pressed for a while.
- You should stay in this position until you see the boot-up screen.

2.6 Connecting To Wi-Fi Network

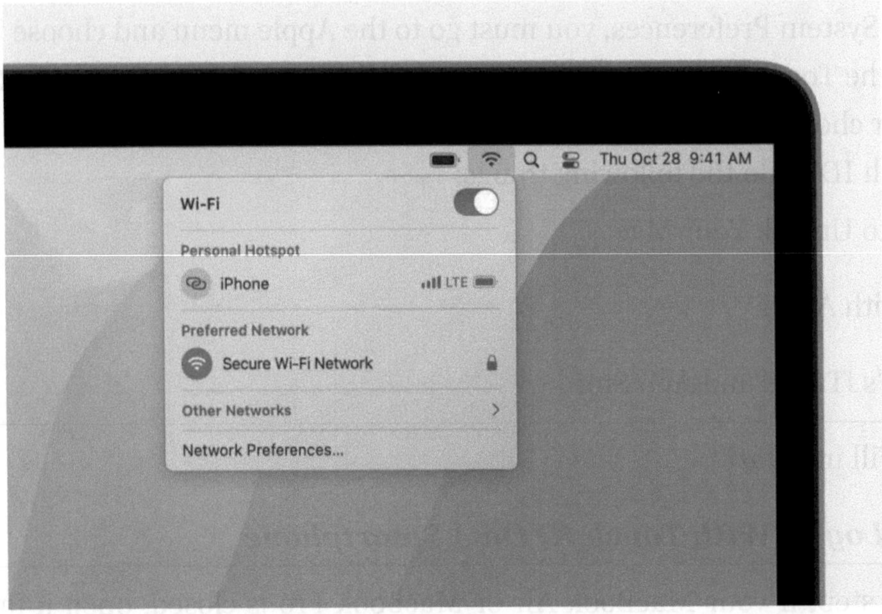

To connect to Wi-Fi using your MacBook, go to the menu bar and click the Wi-Fi icon. After clicking the Wi-Fi icon, select a Network from the menu. You might be asked to enter the Network's password before joining the network. Sometimes, you may be asked to agree to terms and conditions.

There is another way to go about it if you do not see the Wi-Fi icon in the menu bar. Select the **Apple menu**, then go to **System Preferences**. Afterward, click **Network**. On the sidebar, choose **Wi-Fi**, then select **Show Wi-Fi status** in the **menu bar**.

If you want to connect to a hidden Wi-Fi network, select **Other Networks** or **Join Other Network** from the Wi-Fi menu, then select **Other**. Afterward, provide the requested network name, security, and password information.

2.7 Customize The Dock And Menu Bar

The Dock is a minute panel that allows you to quickly access your folders, files, and recently used applications on your Mac. There are changes that you can make to your Dock as well as your Menu Bar if you do not like the way it appears on your Mac. To customize your Dock and Menu Bar, click **System Preferences**, then **Dock and Menu**. You can change your Dock's position, magnification, and size from here. You can add and remove folders by dragging them to and from the Dock and Menu Bar.

2.8 Using Safari

Safari combines the address and search bars for navigating the Internet and conducting searches. It combines these two into one bar called the Smart Search Field. Suggestions for websites as well as search items are provided by the Smart Search Field, thereby making it easy to surf online.

When it comes to navigation, Safari uses three main buttons, which are Back, Forward, and Refresh. The Back and Forward buttons permit you to move through pages you have just viewed earlier. To see your recent history, you can click and hold either button. The Refresh button reloads the current page in cases where the website has stopped working. Sometimes, the Refresh button may act as the Stop button. This happens if a webpage does not load correctly.

2.9 Downloading A File

A file may download automatically if you click its link. However, it may simply open within the browser due to differences in file types. To prevent a file from opening in Safari, use **Save Link As** to download it to your computer directly. To download a file, right-click, then choose **Download Linked File**. The file will start downloading and the progress of the download will be shown in the browser's top-right corner under the **Downloads button**. Once the download is complete, double-click the file to open it.

2.10 Add An Email Account

You will find Mail, Apple's app for sending emails on every Mac. Apple's Mac is a great alternative when you want to access your different emails. This is because it is possible to set it up in a way that allows you to receive all your emails from various email accounts in one place. You will never miss an email again.

To find the Mail app on your Mac, click on the **Mail icon** in the Dock. You could also press **Command** and **Space Bar**, then type in **'Mail.'** Open **System Preferences**, then click on **Internet Accounts**. A list of commonly used services such as iCloud, Google, Facebook, and Yahoo will appear on the right. Click on the + **sign** if you do not see these, then add an email to Mac.

You could also add an email account from within Apple Mail. Open **Mail**, and then go to the menu, click on **Mail,** and choose **Accounts.** This opens the same screen that you get through **System Preferences**. Then add an email to your Mac.

2.11 Add A Printer

There are numerous ways to connect a printer to a Mac. It can be through a wireless connection, IP address, USB, or WPS. You can make a wireless connection through a Bluetooth or Wi-Fi Protected Set-up (WPS). In this section, let's discuss more details on how to add your printer to a MacBook.

2.11.1 Adding A Printer Through WPS

A connection via WPS usually requires you to press the **Wi-Fi** or **Wireless** button on your printer, then the **WPS** button on your router. Please note that steps may vary depending on the type of printer or router that you have. Therefore, you should check for specific router and printer guide instructions. Once you manage to set up WPS, you can progress using the following steps.

On the top left corner of your screen, click the **Apple icon**. Afterward, go to **System Preferences** and click on **Printers and Scanners**. If you are using an older version of Mac, the option for Printers and Scanners is found under Hardware as **Print and Scan**. Click the + **sign** below the list of printers. For an older Mac model, you might have to click **Add Printer or Scanner** after clicking on the + **sign**. It is possible to see the printers your Mac detects under **Nearby Printers** in the Add Printer or Scanner submenu.

Your Mac will display a list of discoverable printers on the network under the **Default tab**. Choose the printer that you would like to add. Go to the **Use field** and select the **printer's** driver or **software**. Finally, click **Add**. The list of printers will be updated, with the new printer added to the list. On the left-hand side of the Print and Scan window, you will see the list of printers available.

2.11.2 Adding A Printer Through The USB

To add a printer via the USB, plug your printer's USB into your Mac desktop or laptop. Click the **Apple icon** and go to **System Preferences**. Afterward, click **Printers and Scanners**. Then, below the list of printers, click the + **sign**. Choose a printer to add. The **Default tab** will give a list of available printers on the network. Then, look for a printer name with USB listed under the column for Kind. Afterward, click **Add** and the printer will be added to the list of printers. The list is on the left-hand side of the Print and Scan window.

2.11.3 Adding A Printer Through The IP Address

Using this step, you need to know your printer's IP address if you want to add a printer. Click the **Apple icon** to find the IP address, then go to **System Preferences**. Click on **Printers and Scanners.** Below the list of printers, click on the + **sign**. Click on the **IP icon**, which looks like a blue globe icon. In the **Address field**, type your printer's IP address. Your Mac will then collect information about the printer. You can rename the printer if you wish. Select the print driver you want to use in the **Use field** and click **Add**.

Chapter 3:

The Basics

3.1 Control Center

Control Center organizes your menu bar extras into a single location, providing quick access to the controls you use most frequently, including Bluetooth, AirDrop, Mic Mode, Screen Mirroring, Focus, and brightness and volume controls. To access the Control Center, click the upper-right corner of the display.

Observe your mic. The recording indicator displays whether or not your computer's microphone is currently in use or was recently used. This indicator light enhances the security and privacy of your Mac by notifying you when an application has access to the microphone.

Click for additional options. Select a button to view additional options. Select the Wi-Fi button, for example, to view your preferred networks, additional networks, or to open Network Preferences. Click again to return to the main Control Center view.

Pin your Control Center favorites. Drag favorite items from Control Center to the menu bar to pin them, allowing for one-click access. To modify what appears in Control Center and the menu bar, open Dock & Menu Bar preferences, select a control from the left pane, and click

"Show in Menu Bar" or "Show in Control Center." You see a preview of the control's position in the menu bar. Certain items cannot be added to Control Center or removed from the menu bar.

To quickly remove an item from the menu bar, hold down the Command key and drag the item away from the menu bar.

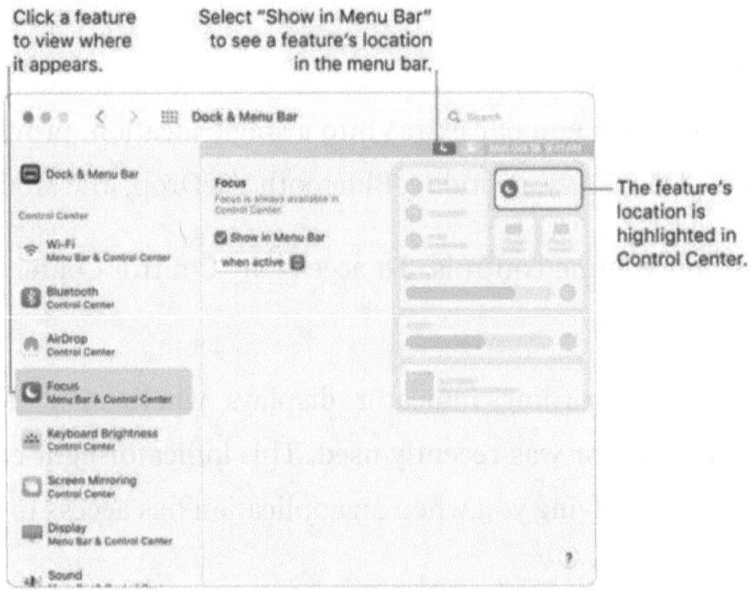

3.2 The Desktop

Have you ever been in a situation where your files are jumbled up all around the desktop? It is important to note that an organized file system is critical to keeping your digital life easier on a Mac. Although Mac has a remarkable search feature that helps you to find files, there are times when you can't remember a file name or may not have given an appropriate name to the document. A particular document may read "untitled document." As such, finding what you are looking for becomes even more difficult.

There are several ways to make a new folder on a Mac. You could create a new folder using **Finder**. To create a new folder via Finder, go to **File** and select **New Folder** in the Finder menu. This folder will appear wherever you are in your Finder file tree.

You could also create a new folder using a trackpad or mouse shortcut. Two-finger tap your **trackpad** or right-click your mouse from your desktop or the finder file system to bring up a menu. The first option is "**new folder**." With this option, you can create a new empty folder wherever you are in the system.

Another way to create order out of desktop chaos is to use the File section. This is usually used for sub-folders. Choose multiple files in a new folder you created from the trackpad or mouse shortcuts mentioned above. This new folder should suffice to house most of the sub-folders that would have been cluttered on your desktop.

Another great way to manage your files is to use the **Spotless application**. You can drag and drop your files onto the application's pop-up drawer in your Menu bar when using Spotless. With Spotless, you can set the rules to sort your files and never again worry about organizing your desktop. In addition, Spotless allows you to create a schedule for organizing files on your desktop according to your preference. This way, the application will automatically organize random files. Spotless is even more interesting in that you can set it to send some items to Trash if need be direct.

3.3 How To Copy, Cut, And Paste

When you want to cut, copy, or paste the text into a document, follow the instructions described in this section. The first step is highlighting the text you want to cut or copy. If you are utilizing a trackpad or mouse, position the cursor at the beginning of the text you want to copy. Afterward, click and hold while dragging the cursor over the text you want to copy.

In cases where you use a keyboard, position the cursor at the beginning of the text you want to copy. After that, press and hold **Shift** while using the keys to select the text you want to copy. Upon completing the highlighting process, a colored box will appear around the selected content.

To copy the highlighted text, press **Command** plus **C** on the keyboard. You could also select **Edit**, then **Copy** from the menu bar. To cut the text, press **Command** and **X** on the keyboard. Also, you could go to the menu bar and choose **Edit**, then **Cut**.

To paste the text, you just cut or copy and position the cursor in an editable area, if they are in a document, or a text box. Press **Command** and **V** on the keyboard or select **Edit**, then **Paste** from the menu bar. Please note that if you want to copy cell contents in Excel, select the cell but not the text, then copy it.

3.4 Keyboard Shortcuts

- Command-O: Open the selected object, or a window to pick a file, if necessary.
- Command-P: Take a printout of the current page.
- Command-S: Take a backup of the current file.
- Command-T: Use another browser window.
- Command-W: Shut the front window. All program windows can be closed by pressing Option-Command-W on a Mac.
- Option-Command-Esc: Force quit an app.

- Command–Space bar: Activate or deactivate the Spotlight search box. For a Spotlight search, press Command–Option–Space bar in Finder. These shortcuts don't show Spotlight if you use various input sources to text in different languages.
- Command-X: The selected object will be cut and copied to the Clipboard for future use.
- Command-C: The selected object may be copied to the Clipboard by pressing Ctrl+C. Use this method to access the Finder as well.
- Command-V: Copy the contents of the Clipboard and paste them into the current document or application. Use this method to access the Finder as well.
- Command-Z: Remove the previous command. To undo the undo command, you can hit Shift-Command-Z. It is possible to undo and redo several actions in some programs.
- Command-A: Select All items.
- Command-F: Open a Find window or search a document.
- Command-G: Discover a previously found item. Shift-Command-G can be used to find the previous occurrence of the word.
- Command-H: The front app's windows will be hidden when this option is selected. Press Option-Command-H to see only the current app and hide all others.
- Command-M: Reduce the size of the Dock's main window. Press Option-Command-M to close all open windows in the current application.
- Control–Command–Space bar: Emojis and other symbols can be selected via the Character Viewer.
- Control-Command-F: If the app allows it, use the app in full-screen mode.
- Space bar: Preview the item you've selected using Quick Look.
- Command-Tab: Open the app that was used the most recently.
- Shift-Command-5: Take a snapshot or capture a video on MacOS Mojave or later. To take a screenshot, press Shift-Command-3 or Shift-Command-4. Find out more about screenshots.
- Shift-Command-N: You may do this by clicking on "New Folder" in your Finder's menu.
- Command-Comma (,): Open the front app's preferences.

3.5 Copying And Pasting Images

Select an image by dragging the cursor over it, then select **Copy Image** from the menu. When you do this, the image goes on to your clipboard. You can now paste the image into any field that accepts them using the step described in the previous section.

3.6 Discover Apps

Wasn't it stressful in the olden days? For example, you need the latest "Call of Duty" game for your Mac. You will have to travel to the brick shop and search through the packages on the store shelves to find them. What if it is not in stock? Then you have to buy it from an online store and go through a lengthy download and installing procedure, or wait for the disc to be shipped - after seven to 10 business days.

However, with the introduction of the **Mac App Store** in January 2011, the time to purchase computer applications from electronics stores is long gone; you can download what you need from the App Store. Some materials are free; others, you have to pay. All you need is an Apple ID and you are done.

Macs come with free, pre-installed software to help you browse the web, create great documents, edit photos and videos, listen to music, and more.

But there are numerous extra apps that you can download from the Mac App Store to give your computer better capacities. They control the range: utilities, games, productivity tools, and everything you can imagine. Thousands of Mac developers present apps from the Mac App Store, which are yours to take.

3.7 Talk To Siri

Siri can be activated by voice on a MacBook Pro and used for various tasks. You can, for instance, schedule meetings, modify preferences, receive responses, send messages, make phone calls, and add events to your calendar. Siri can provide you with directions, e.g., "How do I get to the nearest supermarket?", information "which Mountain is the tallest?", and basic tasks "make a to-do list for me."

If you enable the "Listen for 'Hey Siri'" option in Siri's preferences, Siri will immediately speak to your request whenever you say "Hey Siri."

Note: Your Mac must be connected to the internet to use Siri. Siri may not be accessible in all languages or regions, and features may vary by location.

Activate and enable Siri. Open the System Preferences and click Siri to configure Siri. If Siri was enabled during setup, hold down the Dictation/Siri (F5) key to launch Siri. Or, in System Preferences, click Siri and select Enable Ask Siri. In the Siri pane, you can set additional preferences, such as the language and voice to use and whether Siri should appear in the menu bar.

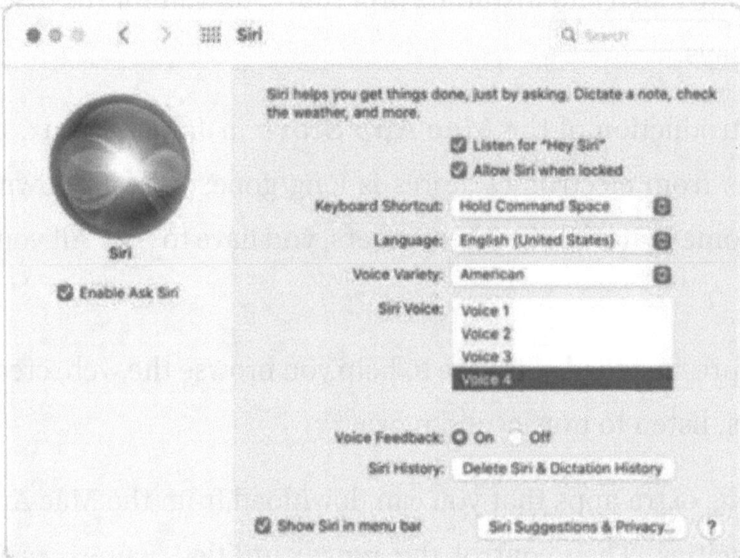

Selecting this option within the Siri section of System Preferences will add the Siri icon to the menu bar. Then hit the Siri icon to enable Siri.

Hey Siri. On MacBook Pro, you can receive responses to your requests by saying, "Hey Siri." To activate this feature in the Siri section of System Preferences, click "Listen for 'Hey Siri'" and then speak multiple Siri commands when prompted.

"**Hey, Siri**" does not respond when the MacBook pro's lid is closed for convenience. You can still activate Siri from the menu bar icon if the lid is closed and an external display is connected.

Perform some music. State "Play some music," and Siri will handle the rest. Even Siri can be instructed to play the most popular song from March 1991.

Drag and drop. You can drag and drop Siri's images and locations into an email, text message, or document. Text can also be copied and pasted.

Replace the voice. Click Siri in System Preferences, then select a Siri Voice menu option.

Throughout this guide, you'll find suggestions for the effective use of Siri; they appear as follows:

Ask Siri. Say something like:

- "Open the Keynote presentation on which I worked last evening."
- "What's the time in London?"

3.8 Use AirDrop To Share Files

For you to send and receive content through Airdrop, you must ensure that Bluetooth and Wi-Fi are turned on and Airdrop is enabled on both devices during the process. So, the device you are sending it from and the device receiving the contents should have their Airdrop, Wi-Fi, and

Bluetooth turned on. For example, if you send an item to an iPhone, you need to ensure the Airdrop, Wi-Fi, and Bluetooth are turned on the iPhone and your MacBook before sending the item. It would be best if you created a Wi-Fi network between the two devices. So, how do you enable Airdrop on your Mac?

1. First, Open Finder. You can click on the Smiley emoji on your Dock to open it.
2. Click on Airdrop at the top left-hand corner of the Finder window. You can click on the **"GO"** option on the menu bar, then select Airdrop.

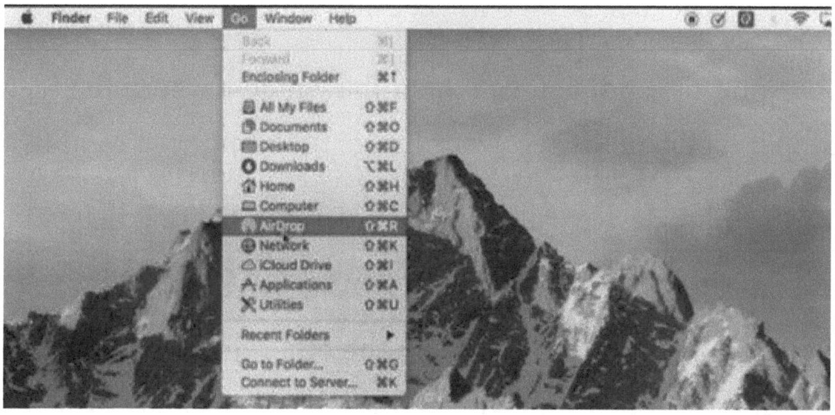

3. Turn on your device Bluetooth and at the bottom of the Airdrop window, you will see **"Allow me to be Discovered by,"** then click the drop-down arrow and choose from the three options. You can choose to be discovered by **"Everyone, Contacts Only, or No One."** It is preferable to choose everyone. When you choose contacts, you will be discovered by only your contacts.

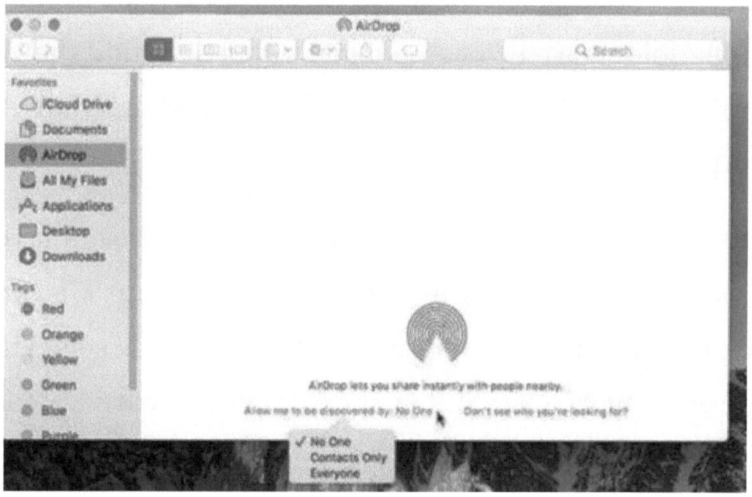

3.8.1 So, How Do You Send and Receive Content?

1. After turning on Airdrop, ensure the other device has its own turned on.
2. So, on the Airdrop window, you will see the available devices to receive and send content.

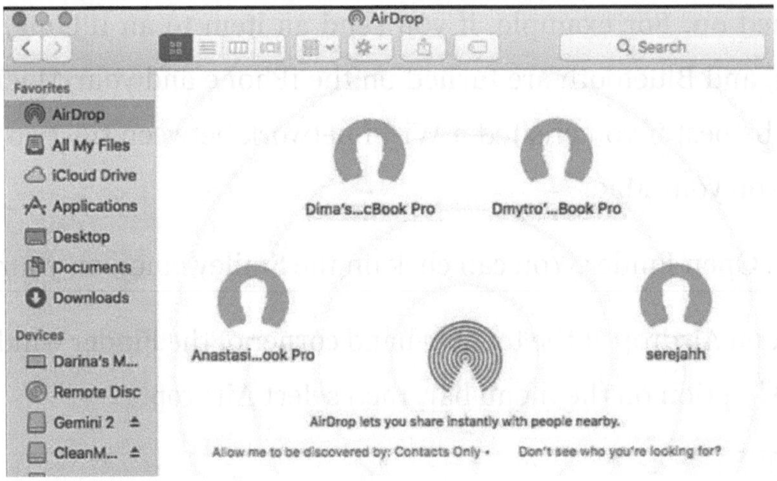

3. Select the file you want to send; you can open the window where the file is located, then drag and drop it on top of the receiver's image (or name) you want to send it to.
4. Once you do that, the other device will get a notification indicating that your MacBook Pro is sending a file to his device. He can choose to Accept or Decline the transfer.
5. The sent file will be in the download folder on the other device. When the download folder of the other device is open, you will see the sent file as it is downloading in the download folder.
6. This is also the same when receiving a file on your MacBook Pro.

3.9 Use AirPlay to Stream Contents

Apple users can use Airplay on their television to watch videos, while playing from their Macs or any other Apple device. To stream a video, connect your device to the same Wi-Fi network as your Airplay 2-compatible smart TV or Apple one. After that, find the video you want to stream and click the **Airplay icon**. The last step should be to select your **Airplay 2-compatible smart TV** or the **Apple one**.

When you are done enjoying your videos and want to stop streaming, click the Airplay icon in the application that you are streaming from, then tap your Mac from the list. Some TV manufacturers have directly incorporated AirPlay 2 into their TV sets. This means you can mirror or share anything from your Mac device to your AirPlay 2- incorporated smart TV.

3.10 Troubleshooting AirDrop And AirPlay Problems

AirDrop has been around for quite a while and has been subject to updates. Even though it has been updated, problems can still come up. Let's look at some of the ways to troubleshoot problems that may arise when using AirDrop in this section.

- Your iPhone may not appear as an AirDrop destination. If this happens, ensure that your hotspot is turned off. To do this, go to **Settings**, then **Personal Hotspot**. AirDrop relies on Wi-Fi and Bluetooth; therefore, interference with either or separation of more than 30 feet between devices can lead to poor performance and an adverse effect on reliability.
- Your Mac may not appear as an AirDrop destination due to inactive Wi-Fi. Ethernet may not be sufficient. Also, check Mac's firewall activity. It might have been set to stop incoming connections if it is active. To correct this issue, go to **System Preferences**, choose **Security and Privacy**, then **Firewall**. Under Firewall are **Firewall options**. Deselect by clicking **Block all incoming connections**.
- For the best results with AirDrop, ensure that you are using the latest versions of Mac OS, iOS, and iPad OS, together with recent Apple hardware.
- You may be asked to accept transfers between your own devices. This means that the devices are not logged in to the same iCloud account.
- There are cases where you can't find a file sent in the destination Downloads folder of Mac because it has retained its original modification and creation dates. It may be sorted differently than expected.

3.11 Sharing Files From iPhone And iPad To MacBook

You can AirDrop documents from your MacBook Pro to another Mac device or an iOS or iPad OS device.

- Launch a Finder window.
- Then, tap a document or folder.
- From the upper section of the Finder window, tap on the Share button.

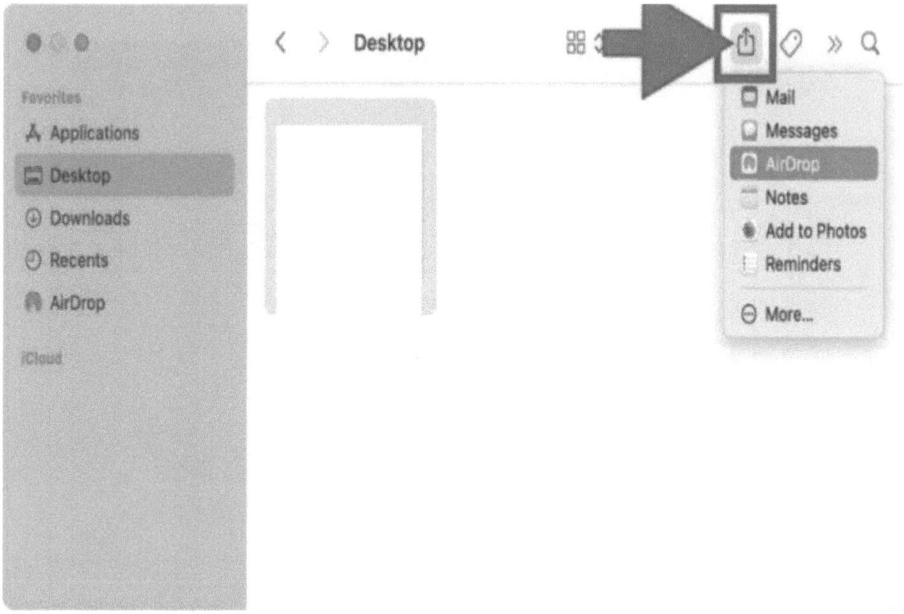

- Then, choose **AirDrop**.

- From there, tap the device you wish to transfer files to and tap twice on the iPhone recipient.

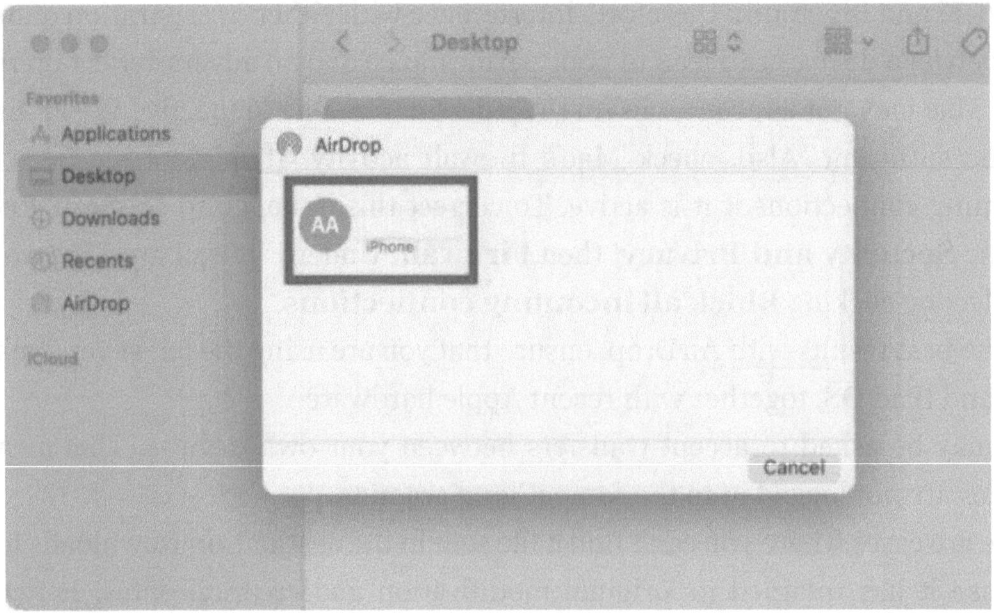

- If you're airdropping an image or movie, it'll be sent to the respective app on the recipient's iPhone.

3.12 Use Apple Pay To Buy Things

Using Apple Pay on your MacBook Pro, you can make purchases on websites simply, securely, and privately. Apple does not store or share your Apple Card or other credit or debit card information with merchants using Apple Pay. When shopping online with Safari, look for Apple Pay as a payment option. Verify payments using Touch ID, your iPhone, or your Apple Watch.

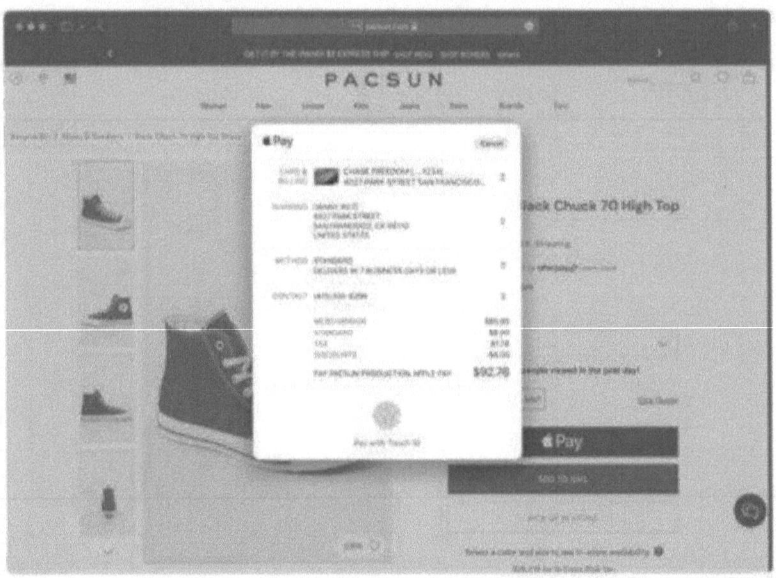

Configure Apple Pay. Apple Pay utilizes the Apple Card or other credit or debit cards you've already added to your iPhone or Apple Watch, so no additional configuration is required. It would be best if you were signed in to an Apple Pay-enabled iPhone or Apple Watch with the same Apple ID used on your MacBook pro. For purchases on your Mac, the default payment card, shipping, and contact information from your iPhone or Apple Watch will be used.

Purchase items using Touch ID. During setup on your MacBook Pro, you are prompted to configure Apple Pay. When using Apple Pay on a website, lightly touch the Touch ID sensor to authenticate and complete the transaction.

Purchase items with your iPhone or Apple Watch. Click the Apple Pay button on the webpage, then use Face ID, Touch ID, or the passcode on your iPhone to confirm the payment, or double-click the side button on your unlocked Apple Watch. It would be best if you were signed in to an Apple Pay-enabled iPhone or Apple Watch with the same ID used on your MacBook pro.

You can manage your Apple Card and add or remove payment cards in the Wallet & Apple Pay section of System Preferences.

Chapter 4:

Customize Your MacBook

4.1 Desktop Wallpaper

Make your Mac more unique by installing a new wallpaper or screen saver. Find out how to do it right here!

Changing your desktop wallpaper or screen saver is a simple way to personalize your Mac and make it feel more like yours. Some people even choose to use their collections of backdrops rather than Apple's pre-installed crop rather than Apple's built-in crop.

4.1.1 How To Install A Pre-Installed Desktop Image On Your Computer

- You can access System Preferences through the Dock or by clicking on the Apple button on your computer's desktop in the upper left corner of your screen. You may also change your desktop background by selecting Change Desktop Background from the context menu when you right-click on the image you're presently using.
- To gain access to the desktop and screen saver, select Desktop & Screen Saver from the Start menu.
- Choose the choice for the desktop.
- Select Desktop Pictures from the Apple menu in the sidebar to open a new window.
- The Desktop Pictures area has several different desktop images.

4.1.2 How To Select An Animated Desktop Background Image

Additionally, you can select a dynamic background that varies throughout the day.

- You can access System Preferences through the Dock or by clicking on the Apple button on your computer's Desktop in the upper left corner of your screen. You may also change your desktop background by selecting Change Desktop Background from the context menu when you right-click on the image you're presently using.
- To gain access to the desktop and screen saver, select Desktop & Screen Saver from the Start menu.
- Choose the choice for the desktop.
- Select Desktop Pictures from the Apple menu in the sidebar to open a new window.
- Choose a desktop background image from the sections Dynamic Desktop or Light and Dark Desktop to use as your desktop background.

4.1.3 How To Use Your Photos As A Background In A Photoshoot

- You can access System Preferences through the Dock or by clicking on the Apple button on your computer's Desktop in the upper left corner of your screen. You may also change your desktop background by selecting Change Desktop Background from the context menu when you right-click on the image you're presently using.
- To gain access to the desktop and screen saver, select Desktop & Screen Saver from the Start menu.
- Choose the choice for the desktop.
- Click the Plus button, which is located at the bottom of the sidebar.
- With a single click, you can select the folder you want to use.
- Choose.
- Select a folder from the sidebar by clicking on the folder's name.
- Choose an image from the directory you've created.

4.1.4 How To Create a Background That Rotates

- You can access System Preferences through the Dock or by clicking on the Apple button on your computer's Desktop in the upper left corner of your screen. You may also change your desktop background by selecting Change Desktop Background from the context menu when you right-click on the image you're presently using.
- To gain access to the desktop and screen saver, select Desktop & Screen Saver from the Start menu.
- Choose the choice for the desktop.
- Choose the location where you'd want your wallpapers to be downloaded.
- Change the image by checking the box next to it.
- You can select the frequency at which you want your backdrop to change.

4.2 Screen Saver

How to install and configure screen savers

- You can access System Preferences through the Dock or by clicking on the Apple button on your computer's Desktop in the upper left corner of your screen. You may also change your desktop background by selecting Change Desktop Background from the context menu when you right-click on the image you're presently using.
- To gain access to the desktop and screen saver, select Desktop & Screen Saver from the Start menu.
- Select the Screen Saver option from the drop-down menu.
- Choose the type of screen saver you want to use.
- Select the source for your screensaver from the Source drop-down menu on the right.
- When your screen saver is ready to begin, press the button.
- Toggle the clock's position on the screen.
- Additionally, you have the option of selecting a random screen saver.

4.3 Mission Control

When using your Mac, fill your screen with many different apps and windows. This is usually a problem if you're on a MacBook with smaller screens than if you're using an iMac. Your screen may look like the image below where you have different windows open and are trying to use them all at once. To do this, you must constantly move windows in front or behind other windows.

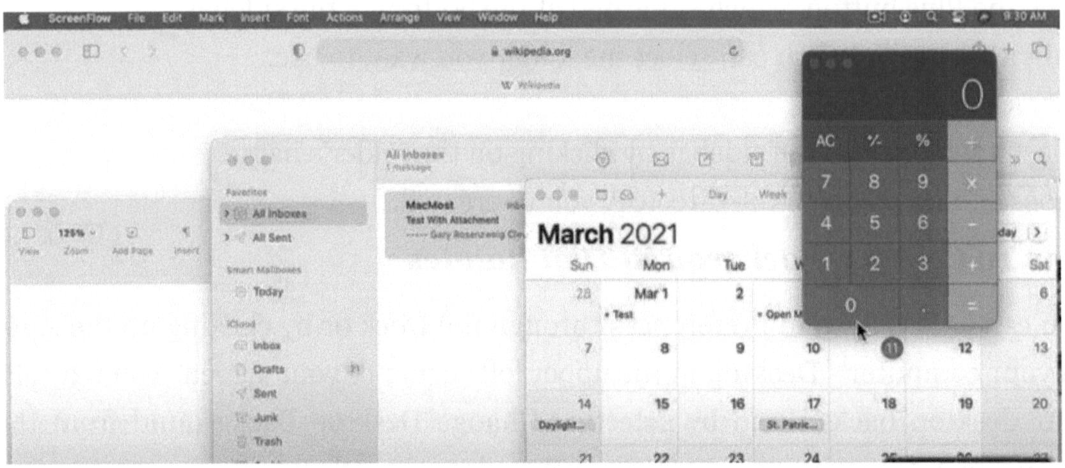

This is where Mission Control comes in. You can use Mission Control to make things easier for you. Mission Control enables you to use multiple desktops. As in the image above, you have just one desktop with many open windows. With Mission Control, you can create another desktop and install some windows. It's like having multiple screens on your Mac. Instead of having multiple physical displays, you will have multiple desktops that you can switch to on your one display.

People use this Mission Control in different ways. Some use the second Desktop to get some irrelevant windows at that moment out of their way and concentrate on something else on the other Desktop. Some use it to make each Desktop specific to a task they are doing. For example, you may have Notes, Pages, and a Safari window all on one Desktop because you're surfing the web and writing a paper or books simultaneously. You can have it on the other Desktop, Reminders, Mail, and Calendar because that's where you go to check your emails, schedule events, etc. below are some things you can do with Mission Control.

1. To activate Mission Control, you can use the **Control key** + the **Up-Arrow key**. You can use the shortcut key, which is the **F3 key**. You can press the F3 key, hold down the Fn key, and then press F3.
2. This will bring up **Mission Control**. As you can see in the image below, the first thing it does is to take all the windows and move them apart. At the top, it shows you that you have one Desktop. When you move your cursor there, it will expand and show you what the Desktop looks like.

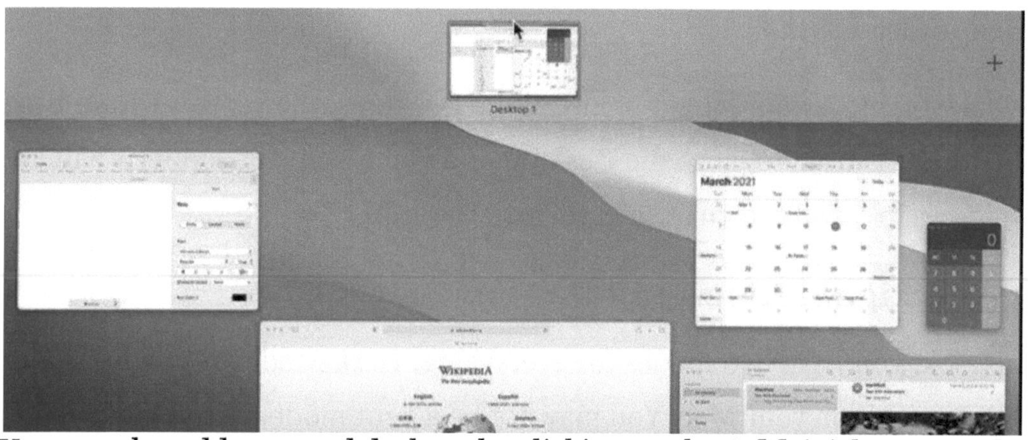

3. You can also add a second desktop by clicking on the **Add (+)** button at the top right-hand side of the screen. You will see Desktop 1 and 2 at the top of the menu when you click on them. Desktop 2 will be empty.

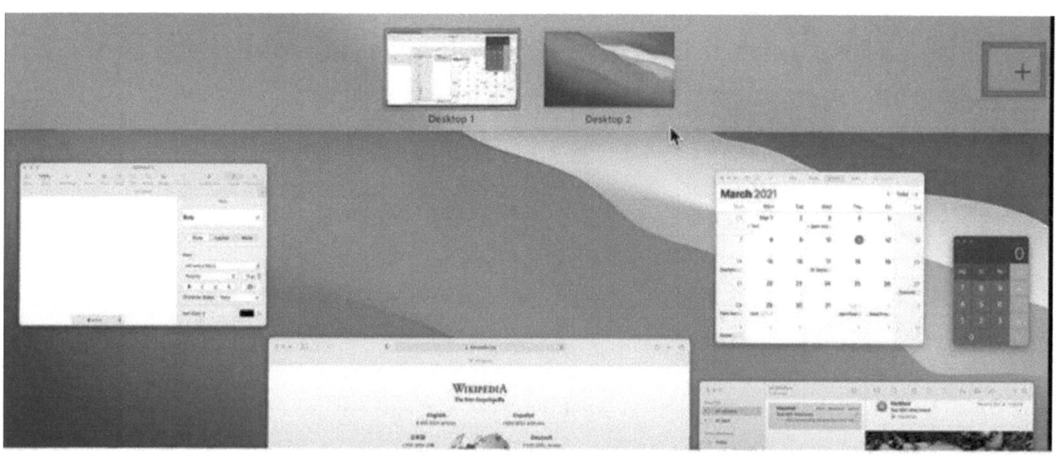

4. You can add some of the windows to Desktop 2. To add them, drag the window you want to add and drop it inside the desktop. You can go into each desktop by clicking on the desktop. You can add more Desktops if you want.

5. You can use keyboard shortcuts to switch between Desktops quickly. Use **The Control key + The Left and Right Arrow keys** to switch between two Desktops. The Control key + Left Arrow key takes you to the first Desktop while The Control key + Right Arrow key takes you to the second Desktop.

6. You can use a gesture to do this using your **Trackpad**. To do this, use four fingers on the Trackpad and swipe left or right to quickly switch between Desktops. There's a setting for this gesture in System Preferences. Open your **System Preferences** > Click on **Trackpad** > click on the **More Gestures Tab** > Check the box where it says **"Swipe between full-screen apps."**

7. In Mission Control, you can move the Desktops around and rearrange them into the order you want. You can make Desktop 1 become Desktop 2 by dragging the Desktop to the order you want.

8. When you move your cursor to any of the Desktops, there's this **Close button (X)** at the top. It is used to close the Desktop and when you click on it, it will close and the windows in it will return to the previous Desktop.

4.4 Dark And Light Mode

On your MacBook, you have two modes for everything: Dark Mode and Light Mode. The Light mode comes by default on your Mac. You may not be a light mode person and would love to use the dark mode. You can change this in the System Preferences. Simply,

- Open your **System Preferences** and click on **General.**
- In the General pane, on the Appearance option, select **Dark Mode**.
- You can also choose to set it to **Auto**. This will give you light mode in the daytime and Dark mode at night.

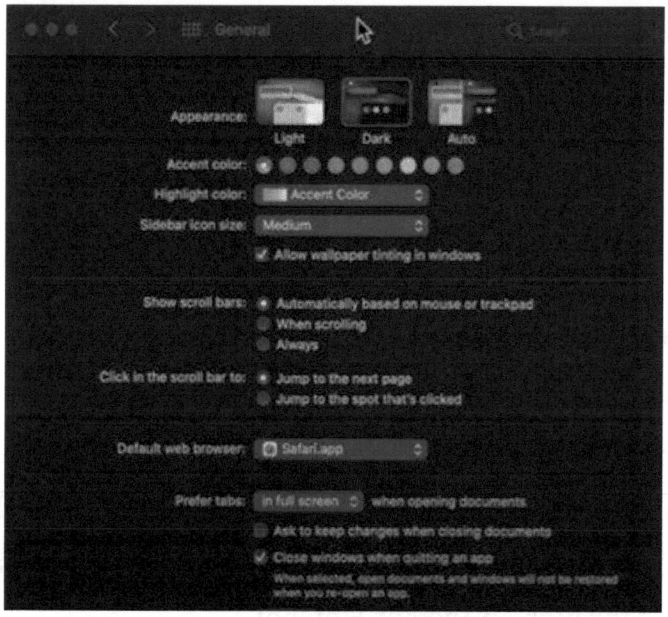
General
Appearance:
Light
Dark
Auto
Accent color:
Highlight color:
Accent Color
Sidebar icon size:
Medium
Allow wallpaper tinting in windows
Show scroll bars:
Automatically based on mouse or trackpad
When scrolling
Always
Click in the scroll bar to:
Jump to the next page
Jump to the spot that's clicked
Default web browser:
Safari.app
Prefer tabs:
in full screen
when opening documents
Ask to keep changes when closing documents
Close windows when quitting an app
When selected, open documents and windows will not be restored when you re-open an app.

Chapter 5:

Internet And Apps

5.1 Basics Of Using the Internet

5.1.1 Connect Your Mac to The Internet Via A USB Cable.

It is now simple to connect to the Internet from your Mac, whether at home, at work, or on the go. The two most common means of connecting to the Internet are a Wi-Fi (wireless) connection and an Ethernet (wired) connection. If neither of these alternatives is available, you may be able to connect to the Internet through an Instant Hotspot.

5.1.2 Make Use Of Wi-Fi.

Whenever there is a Wi-Fi network available, the Wi-Fi icon appears in the top menu bar of the computer. To connect to a network, click on the symbol and choose one. In this case, a lock symbol displays next to the network name, indicating that the network is password-protected; in this case, you must enter the password before connecting to the Wi-Fi network.

5.1.3 Make Use Of Ethernet.

Networking can be accomplished through the use of an Ethernet network or the use of a DSL or cable modem. You should connect a network cable to the Ethernet port on your Mac, which is signified by the asterisk (). If your Mac does not have an inbuilt Ethernet port, you can connect the Ethernet cable to a USB or Thunderbolt port on your computer by using an adapter to link the cable to the computer. How to connect to an Ethernet network is explained in detail.

5.1.4 Make Use Of An Instant Hotspot.

Using your Mac and Instant Hotspot, you may be able to connect to the internet using your iPhone or iPad's hotspot if you don't have access to Wi-Fi or Ethernet at your location.

Your internet service provider may provide a Wi-Fi or Ethernet connection when you're at home, depending on your location. If you are unsure your access, you should contact your Internet service provider.

Depending on your place of employment, you may have access to a Wi-Fi or Ethernet network connection. Information technology departments or network administrators at your firm can provide specifications on how to connect to and use the network and information on network usage guidelines.

Using Wi-Fi hotspots (public wireless networks) or your Mac's Instant Hotspot while traveling is a convenient way to stay connected while on the go (if your Mac and your phone carrier support it). However, it would be best if you remembered that to access some Wi-Fi hotspots, you may be required to submit a password, agree to the terms of service, or pay a fee.

5.2 Using Safari

There are many web browsers that you can use to stay in touch with your loved ones. In addition to Safari, there is Google Chrome, Opera, and Mozilla. However, the best way to enjoy the internet on your Apple devices is to use the Safari browser. Safari outperforms many other browsers in terms of how it functions. To make Safari your default browser on a Mac, select the **Apple menu**, choose **System Preferences**, then click **General**. Afterward, a pop-up menu will appear, from which you should click the **Default Web Browser** option, then select **Safari**.

5.3 Check Your Mail

In Mac Mail, the quickest way to manually check for new email messages is to press **Command**, **Shift**, and **N** on your keyboard. Another way is to click on the **Mailbox** menu, then select **Get All New Mail**. There is yet another way that you can use to access your iCloud email on a Mac; open your **Finder**, click **Applications**, then select **System Preferences**. If prompted, Sign in with your Apple ID, username, and password. Otherwise, you may need to double-click the **Apple ID** icon. Click the **blue box** next to the Mail option, if it has not been selected. Afterward, close the **System Preferences** window, then click the **Mail App** icon in your Dock.

It is also possible to check your iCloud email on the iCloud Website. The first step is to visit **iCloud.com**. Afterward, sign in using your username and password. Suppose you have not signed into iCloud.com before; it is important to follow the verification prompts so that the iCloud Website gets access to your account data. Select the **Mail** symbol. Make sure your Mail is turned on in your iOS settings to access your messages.

5.4 Chat Using Messages

It is possible to send unlimited messages to any iPod touch, iPad, iPhone, and Mac using Apple's secure-messaging service called iMessage. To send a message, open **Messages**; after this, you might be asked to sign in with your Apple ID. You can then click the **New Message** button, which you will find at the top of the Messages Window. To send messages to the recipients, type their name, phone number, and email address. Alternatively, you could click the **Add** button and choose recipients from your contacts list. To type your message, press **Tab** or go to the bottom of the window and click the message field.

If you want to include an emoji, image, or audio recording, there are ways to go about it. For example, to include an audio recording, go to the **Record audio** button and then say your message. Go ahead and click the **Emoji Picker** button if you wish to include an emoji. Press **Return** to send the message.

5.5 FaceTime Call from Messages

When conversing with an individual or a group, it is feasible to start a FaceTime call. FaceTime is an application that allows you to make voice and video calls over the internet. It is a great application for keeping in touch with your loved ones who use Apple devices. On the upper-right corner of the window, in macOS Monterey, click the **FaceTime** button and select **FaceTime Video** or **FaceTime Audio**. You could also go to the window's upper-right corner and click **Details**, before clicking the FaceTime audio or video button.

5.6 Making A Call With FaceTime

Interestingly, with advances in technology, you can now receive or make a phone call in an area with little or no cellular coverage. All you have to do is connect to a Wi-Fi network. Turn on Wi-Fi calling in **Settings** to place Wi-Fi calls from your iPhone. Click on **Phone**, then **Wi-Fi calling**. For emergency services, you might need to confirm or enter your address. In the status bar, you will see the option Wi-Fi after your carrier name if the Wi-Fi-calling service is available. Please note that when there is a cellular service, your iPhone utilizes it for emergency calls. In cases where you turn on Wi-Fi calling and the cellular service is unavailable, emergency calls might use Wi-Fi calling.

5.7 Take A Selfie With Photo Booth

It is possible to take a selfie with Photo Booth using your Apple device. Let's talk more about the photo booth so that you understand what exactly it is. A photo booth can be described as a portable kiosk that is used for snapping pictures of you and your friends in front of a backdrop. In simple terms, a photo booth could be described as an entertaining and easy way to create memories, filling the silence at your event, be it a party, wedding, or any other joyous moment. The booths are exposed or enclosed, depending on the vendor you get them from.

Let's discuss how you can use your Mac to take photos. You can capture an individual or group of four photos on your Mac. You can also record a video using the built-in camera on your machine. Another possibility is the use of an external video camera that is connected to your Mac.

To take a photo using an external video camera, ensure it is connected to your computer. Also, make sure that the camera is turned on. Go to the **Photo Booth app** on your Mac and then to the **View Photo** button. Afterward, click the **Take Photo** button. If you want to take a single photo, go to the bottom left of the window and click the click the **Take four quick pictures** option to take a still picture button. For a sequence of four photos,. These four photos are also known as "4-up photos." Finally, click on the **Take Photo** option.

5.8 Recording A Video Using Photo Booths

Sometimes you may be eager to let your loved one know exactly how certain events unfold. It is possible to capture important events when they occur. Consider a situation where a baby starts to have its first steps. Although a loved one may not be able to see this as it happens, a video recording will come in handy in making them also experience the joy of seeing their baby walk for the first time.

If you have to record a video using an external video camera, ensure to connect it to the computer. Do not forget to turn on the camera. Go to the **Photo Booth app** and click on the **View Video** button when using your Mac. Afterward, click the **Record Video** button. Sometimes, the Record Video button may not show. In this case, go to the bottom left and click **Record a movie clip** button. When you are done capturing your precious moment, click the **Stop** button.

5.8.1 Applying An Effect In Photo Booth On Mac

Photo Booth has functionalities for adding some fun effects to your videos and photos. To apply effects on your Mac, go to the **Photo Booth** app. Click on **Take Photo** or **Record Video.** Afterward, on the bottom right, click on **Effects**. To see the preview of the available effects, click the browse buttons at the bottom of the window. Afterward, select and click the effect that you prefer. When you move the pointer over the image, a slide with some distortion effects will appear. Go ahead and move the slider if you want to see how the distortion can change the photo or video. You can then select the distortion that gives the changes you are looking for.

If the effects do not look appealing to you, they can do away with them so that the photo or video becomes normal again. In the middle role of effects, select **Normal**, then click the **Take Photo** or **Record Video** option. When the recording is complete, click the **Stop** button.

5.9 Viewing Photos on Mac

Go to the photo booth app on your Mac and select a thumbnail. Click one of the photos to have a larger view when viewing a 4-up photo. To view all four photos, click again on the photo that allows you to have a larger view. In cases where you want to see a slideshow of the photos, select **View**, click on **Start Slideshow**, then utilize the controls at the bottom of the screen.

5.10 Check Your Stocks

The Stocks application is the best way to monitor the market on your Mac. View prices in the custom watchlist, click a stock to view more information and an interactive chart and read market-moving Apple News articles.

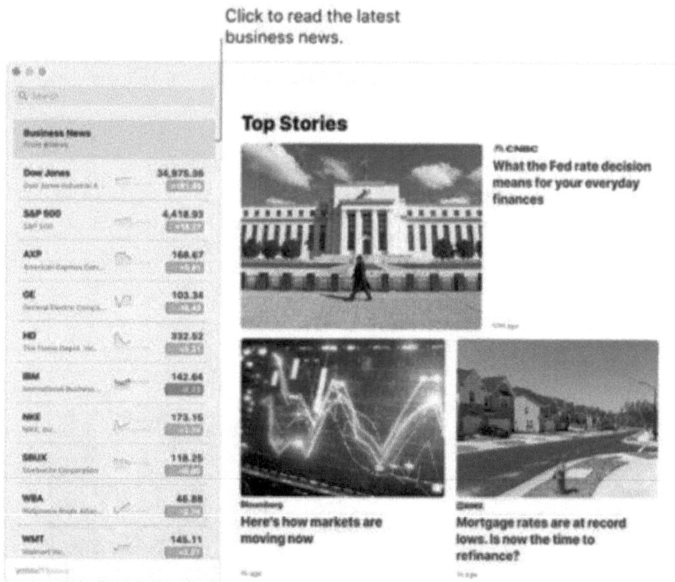

Apple News articles and Top Stories are accessible in the United States, Canada, the United Kingdom, and Australia. Yahoo provides news articles from other nations and regions.

Personalize your watchlist In the Search field: To personalize your watchlist in the search field follow the following steps;

1. enter a company name or symbol to add a stock to your watchlist.
2. Double-click the stock symbol in the search results to view stock information.
3. Click the Add to Watchlist button in the upper-right corner to add the stock to your watchlist.

To remove a stock from the Watchlist, Control-click the symbol and select "Remove from Watchlist." Control-clicking security in your watchlist will open it in a new tab or window.

Examine market changes: Click the green or red button below each price on your watchlist to toggle between price change, percentage change, and market capitalization. The watchlist also contains color-coded sparklines that track daily performance.

Read articles about the companies that you are following. Click a stock on your watchlist to view an interactive chart, additional information, and the most recent news for that company. Apple News has curated a collection of timely business articles, which can be accessed by selecting Business News at the top of the watchlist.

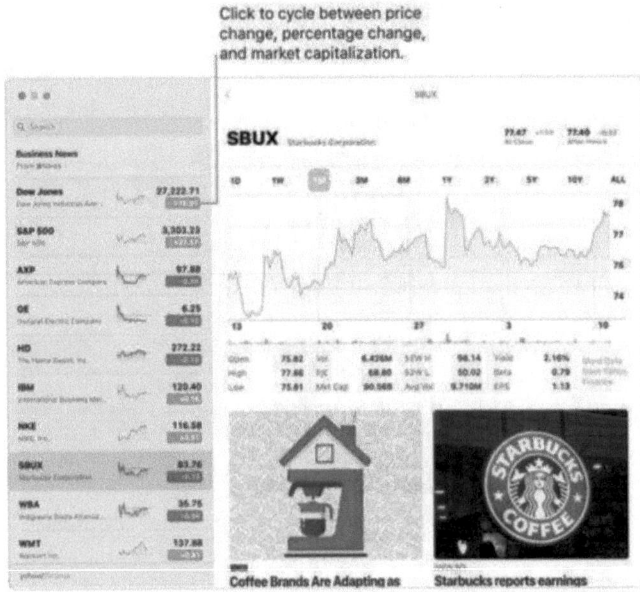

Get a deeper view. Want to know how the market performed last week, month, or year? Click the buttons atop the chart to switch timeframes and view prices from your preferred perspective.

Your watchlist is accessible on all of your devices: When you sign in to all of your devices with the same Apple ID, your watchlist will remain consistent.

5.11 How To Export Photos and Videos

If you want to use your videos and photos in other apps, you can Export them. Video clips are Exported as MOV files, while 4-up and single photos are exported as JPEG ones. In the Photo Booth app on your Mac, export a video clip or photo by selecting the **thumbnail**. Afterward, select **File**, then **Export**. In the case of a 4-up photo, choose the **photo frame**, then **File**, before clicking **Export**. To export a non-effect photo, choose the thumbnail, then select **File** and **Export Original**.

In addition to exporting photos and videos, there are other ways to share them from Photo Booth. These include sharing through Messages, Mail, AirDrop, Notes, Reminders, and Add to Photos. Still in your Photo Booth app, choose the **photo or video thumbnail**s you wish to share. Click the **Share** button prior to choosing how to share them. If you choose **Messages**, for example, the photo or video will be inserted in a new text message.

If you share your photos or videos through Mail, they will be inserted into a new email. AirDrop is another option for sharing. The Photo Booth app will list other people who are utilizing AirDrop. To share the files with them, click their names. Choosing 'Notes' will make the photos and videos to be inserted in a new note, whereas the "Add to Photos" option adds them to your Photos library. Photos and videos are inserted in a new reminder if you select 'Reminders'.

Chapter 6:

Photos And Media

6.1 View And Edit Your Photos

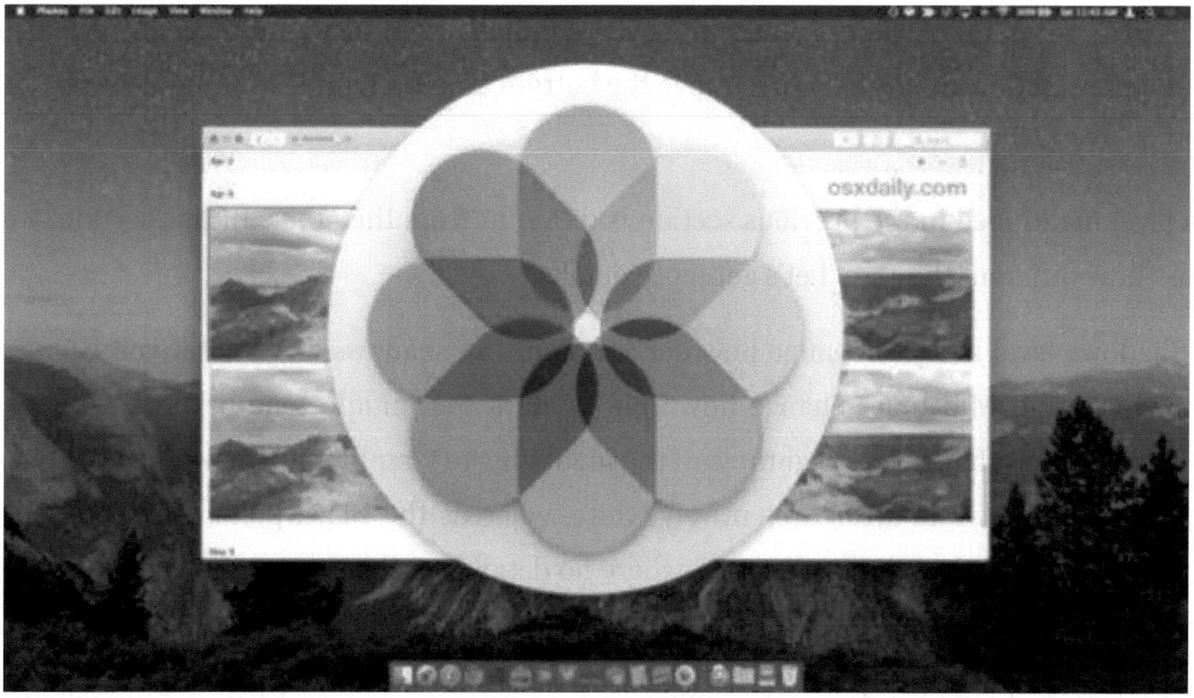

Photos allow you to rate, view, group, and store images on your Mac. You can easily add photos to your iCloud library and sync them with all of your devices through iCloud. If you 'like' certain images in Photos, they are automatically added to your favorites. With its grouping feature, Photos makes it easier for you to find certain pictures when needed. The Photos app allows for face detection. It allows you to see a certain individual's photos that are in your Mac.

Photo-editing tools can easily be used to make simple changes to your photos. Such changes include rotating them, as well as cropping them to get the best framing. There are also vast adjustments that can be made to change color and exposure, eliminate red-eye, change white balance, and remove blemishes or marks, to mention a few. It is possible to make further adjustments by using **Levels** and **Curves** controls to change contrast, brightness, and tonal range in different areas of the same photo. You can also change and improve videos and live photos.

6.1.1 Applying Levels Adjustments To A Photo

You can alter the settings levels to darken or lighten areas and change the contrast in a photo. You can adjust settings for the shadows, highlights, mid-tones, and white and black points. The appearance of specific colors can also be changed. To apply level adjustments to a photo on your Mac, go to the **Photos app**, double-click a photo, and click **Edit**. In the toolbar, click **Adjust**, then the arrow next to Levels. To automatically correct the adjustment levels of a photo, click the pop-up menu below Levels, select **Luminance**, **RGB**, or the color you wish to alter. Afterward, click **Auto**. To manually adjust levels, drag the handles of the histogram to make the desired adjustments. Option-drag a handle to move the bottom and top handles simultaneously.

6.1.1.1 The Different Levels Available

Each level mentioned in the previous section is different from the other. In this section, we will discuss how different they are. Let's get more details.

The Shadows level lets you change how dark or light the shadows are so that you can see the details you want. Mid-tones change how light or dark the middle-tone parts of a photo are. Highlights let you change the brightness of the highlights to your liking. The white point changes the level at which white areas are entirely white, whereas the Black point alters the latter to become completely black, up to the point where no detail is visible.

6.1.2 Applying Curves Adjustments To A Photo

On your Mac, go to the **Photos app**, double-click a **photo**, then click **Edit**. In the toolbar, click **Adjust**, go to the **Adjust pan**e, and then click the arrow next to **Curves**. To automatically correct the curves of a photo, click the pop-up menu below Curves. Select **RGB** or the color that you wish to correct. Afterward, click **Auto**. To manually adjust a photo's color curves, click the **Add points** option and then click the areas on the photo that you wish to change. With each click, points are added to the histogram's diagonal line. You can also add points by clicking along the histogram's diagonal line. Once you finish adding the points, drag the points to alter the contrast and brightness in the photo.

When you alter a video or photo, Photos preserves the original so that you can always undo your changes and return to the old, natural look. The alterations you make to a video or photo will appear everywhere, in your library, project, or every other album on your Mac. Suppose you wish to give a photo or video an exceptional look that only appears in one version of the item; duplicate it, then work on the copy.

To edit a video or photo on your Mac, go to the **Photos app** and double-click a **photo or video thumbnail**. Afterward, click **Edit** in the toolbar. Select a video thumbnail or photo, then press

Return. The Edit toolbar shows a Zoom slider and buttons for making changes, cropping photos, adding filters, enhancing, and rotating photos.

To adjust a photo, click **Adjust**. By clicking the adjust option, the adjustment tools will be displayed. From there, you can make the necessary ones that you wish to. Zooming in or out on a photo is done by dragging or clicking the Zoom slider. To apply filters on a photo, click **Filters**, whereas if you want to crop, select **Crop** so that the cropping options are displayed.

Rotating a video or photo is done by clicking the **Rotate** button in the toolbar. Go ahead and continue clicking until you get your desired orientation. To automatically enhance a video or photo, click the **Auto Enhance** button to get an automatic adjustment of the contrast and color. If you wish to remove the changes, click **Revert to Original** or Press **Command** and **Z** on your keyboard. Once you finish the editing process, click **Done** or press **Return**.

6.1.3 Duplicating A Photo

As we mentioned, if you want to create different versions of a video or photo, you should first duplicate it. Afterward, you can then work on the copy. To duplicate an item on your Mac, go to the **Photos app** and select the photo you want to copy. Select **Image**, then **Duplicate 1 Photo**. Instead of clicking on **Duplicate 1 Photo**, you could also press **Command** and **D**. For a live photo, click **Duplicate** to include the video portion. For the still image, click **Duplicate as Still Photo**.

6.2 Listen To Music

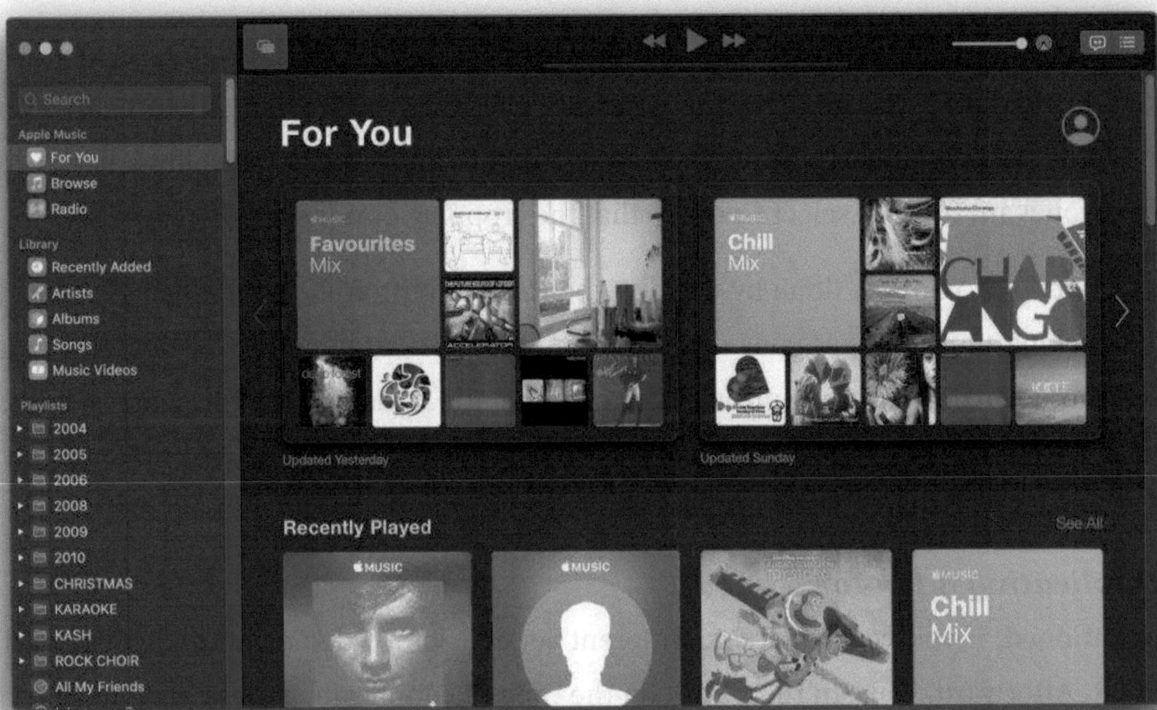

In the Music app on your Mac, you can find music in your music library. To find a particular album or song, click any option below **Library** in the sidebar on your left. For instance, click **Albums** to view all the albums available in your library. To choose a playlist, go to the sidebar on the left and select a playlist below **Playlists**. You can move the pointer over any song or album; then click the Play button. You can shuffle, repeat, play songs in a particular order, fade between songs, and use the **Playing Next** queue when listening to your music.

6.2.1 Using The Music App For Mac

The Apple Music part of the Music app is grouped into three key sections, which are Listen Now, Browse, and Radio. You can use the sidebar to navigate through them; from your **Applications Folder** or **Dock**, open **Music**. In the sidebar, click **Listen Now** to see what your friends have been listening to, recently played playlists and albums, your Apple-curated mixes, and suggestions. Still on the sidebar, click Browse to see currently-trending artists, Apple's curated playlist selections, new music, and the rest of Apple Music's available library.

On the sidebar, you could also click **Radio** to view and play **Apple Music 1 radio shows**, both previously recorded as well as those who are live at any given moment. Click **Music Country**, **Music Hits**, or **Music 1** in the Radio section to view and play content from those Radio stations.

6.2.2 Importing Music Into The Music App

To import music into the Music app:

1. Go to your **Dock** or **Applications** folder and open **Music**.
2. In the **Menu Bar**, click **File**, then **Import**.
3. Select the folder or file that you want to import and click **Open**.

6.3 Read Books

Utilize Apple Books on Mac to read and organize your library of books and audiobooks and purchase new titles. Establish reading objectives and track what you wish to read and what you are currently reading.

Your Mac's library: The books you've begun reading appear first in **Reading Now**. Browse or search on all the items in your library, click Book Store or Audiobook Store in the sidebar and select a category to discover new books and other publications. Sign in with your Apple ID to purchase an item. Additionally, you can buy books directly from the search results.

Ask Siri. Say something like, "Find Jane Austen's works."

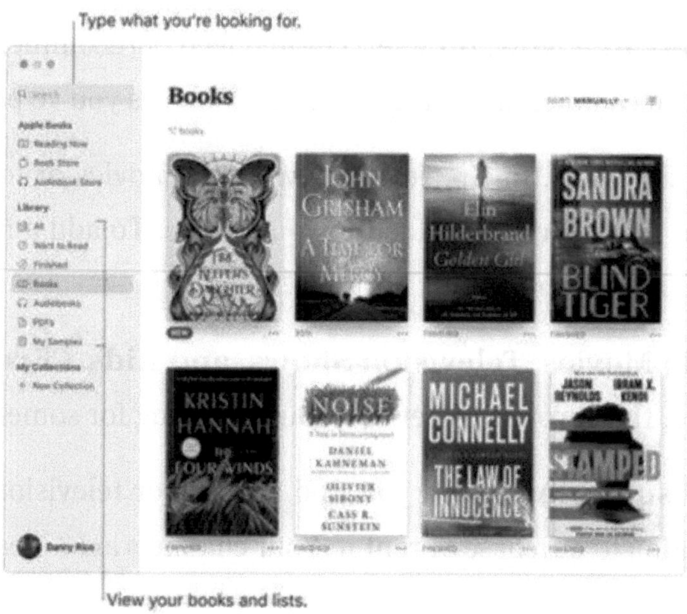

Set reading objectives: Set daily reading goals to increase your motivation to read. Click in the Reading Goals section of Reading Now and select a new goal if you want to increase the default daily reading time of five minutes. You can disable this feature and clear your reading goal data in the Books preferences.

Add bookmarks, highlights, and notes. To bookmark, a page, move the cursor to the top of the book to reveal the controls, then click (click the bookmark again to remove the bookmark). To visit a bookmarked page, click to display the controls, then click the bookmark.

To add highlights or notes, select the text, then select a highlight color or Add Note from the menu that appears. To view your notes later, display the controls and click .

Never lose your position or your annotations. As long as you are signed in with the same Apple ID on your Mac, iOS devices, and iPadOS devices, your purchased books, collections, bookmarks, highlights, and notes, as well as the current page you are reading, are automatically synced.

Modify the theme to Night for easier reading in low-light conditions. Select View > Theme > Night, or click the Appearance AA, followed by the black circle. Not every book has a Night theme.

6.4 Watching TV & Movies

Utilize the Apple TV application to watch all of your movies and television shows. Purchase or rent movies and television programs, subscribe to channels and continue watching on any of your devices from where you left.

Start watching with Watch Now. Browse a curated feed of recommendations in Watch Now based on your subscribed channels and the movies or TV shows you've previously viewed.

Continue watching Up Next. In Up Next, you will find movies or television shows you are currently watching and those you have added to your queue. To add a new movie or television show to Up Next, click the Add to Up Next button.

Explore more within Movies, Television Shows, and Kids. Click the Movies, TV Shows, or Kids tab in the menu, then browse by genre if you're looking for something specific.

Purchase, lease, or subscribe. When you find a movie or television program you want to watch, you have the option to purchase or rent it. Your channels are accessible on all devices and can be shared with up to six family members via Family Sharing.

Check out what your peers are sharing. When your friends and family use the Messages app to send you TV shows and movies, you can view them at your convenience. Look for them in the Apple TV app, in the new Shared With You section of Watch Now. Content appears in Shared with You only if the sender is listed in your Contacts.

Choose an item from your library. Click Library to see your purchased and downloaded movies and TV shows organized by genre. To begin watching, click the movie or television show.

6.5 QuickTime And VLC

The first choice for Mac users is QuickTime Player. This is because it is bundled with Mac OS X. It is better to choose VLC Media Player if you are a Windows user. The major difference between the two players is that QuickTime Player can play iTunes M4V movies, whereas VLC Media Player cannot directly play M4V movies.

Non-Apple devices such as VLC Media Player cannot play iTunes M4V movies because the iTunes M4V movies have Digital Restriction Management (DRM) protection, a technology that controls what you can do with the devices and digital media that you possess. However, if you are interested in enjoying iTunes movies on VLC Media Player, you can download NoteBurner M4V Converter Plus, a powerful DRM removal tool. NoteBurner M4V Converter Plus can record iTunes purchases and rentals. Once you remove the iTunes DRM, you can convert movies to different formats such as AVI, MOV, and MP4.

Apple developed an extendable multimedia framework called QuickTime Player. You can get it for free using OS X and Windows operating systems. QuickTime Player handles various digital video formats, sound, picture, interactivity, and panoramic images. One of the main features of the QuickTime Player is that it fully supports Mac OS X. Also, QuickTime Player can save existing QuickTime movies directly to a hard disk drive from the web. QuickTime also encodes and transcodes audio and video from one format to the other. In addition, QuickTime can save the embedded video in a *.mov file format or its original format no matter what the origins are. Other video players you can use to watch videos on your Mac include Wondershare Filmora, 4.5K Player, Cisdem VideoPlayer, MPlayerX, and Elmedia Player.

Chapter 7:

Maps & Reminders

7.1 How To Use Maps To Explore The World

You can explore the world using the Maps app on Mac. The application allows you to get directions for walking, cycling, public transportation, and driving. For quick access on the go, you may as well send directions to your Apple Watch, iPad, or iPhone.

In the Maps app on your Mac, click the Directions button in the toolbar. Afterward, enter your current location and destination. Click your destination—for example, a pin on a map or a landmark—before clicking the Directions in the place card. Maps use your current location as your starting point. However, it is possible to enter a different one. The Swap Directions button allows you to swap your starting and finishing points. Depending on your preferences, you can click the Walk, Drive, Bicycle, or Transit button. To see the list of possible directions that you can take, click the Trip Details button.

If you are driving, note that directions can include electric vehicle routing, congestion zones, and license plate restrictions. You can keep track of your current charge if your vehicle is compatible. You could also see charging stations that are along your way. The Maps app can give you a heads-up on congested zones when you are in major cities such as Paris, Singapore, and London. This helps reduce traffic in dense areas by providing you with routes around the congested zones.

Regarding license plate restrictions, some Chinese cities that limit access to dense areas. The Maps app can help you get around or through a restricted area based on your eligibility.

Depending on your city, directions can be provided if you are bicycling. You can choose when to depart or arrive by public transportation and driving. Simply click Plan to choose when you want to leave or arrive. To close the directions list, click again on the Trip Details button.

7.1.1 Showing The 3d Map In Maps

By utilizing the 3D tool in the Maps app, you can get a more realistic view of a certain location. The application has a way of simulating building structures so that you can get a more detailed idea of how the area looks. Once you have enabled the 3D map, remember to zoom in close so that you can really see what it is capable of doing. From the **Dock** or **Finder**, launch the **Maps** app. In the bottom left corner of the Maps window, click **Show**, then Show **3D Map**. From there, you can click and drag the 3D icon that you find at the bottom right corner of the screen. This helps you to decrease or increase your view of the 3D buildings. To rotate your view, click and drag the compass in a circular motion. The compass is at the bottom right corner of the screen.

7.1.2 Using The Flyover

The Maps development team at Apple has given special attention to some destination spots worldwide. Flyover is an exceptional feature that allows you to have a visual adventure across a city. You will have an opportunity to fly around, looking at iconic spots such as Buckingham Palace in London and the Eiffel Tower in Paris. Go to your **Dock** or **Finder** to open the **Maps app**. Search for a **Flyover** city, then enter a location. Next to the **3D Flyover Tour** tab at the bottom center of the screen, click the **Start** option. Once you click on the Start option, you will be taken on a visual adventure across the city. Click on **End** when you are done enjoying and want to stop the tour.

7.2 Planning A Route

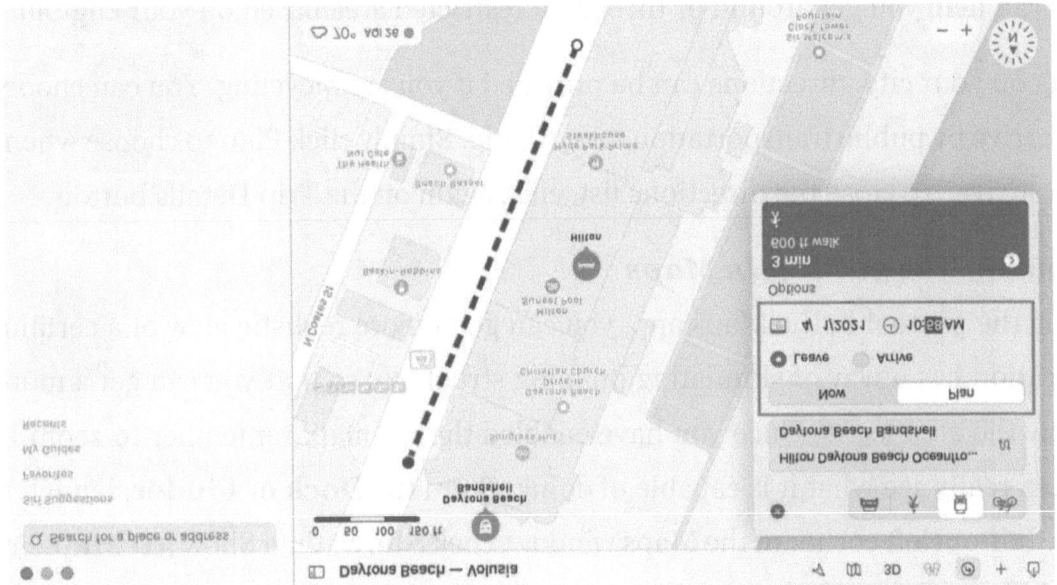

It is crucial to plan a route on your Mac before a cycling day or a big trip. Ensure you are signed in on your device and on your Mac with the same Apple ID. This will allow you to share the details with another device. To plan a route on your Mac, you should follow the next steps. On your Mac, go to the Maps app and click a location on the map, be it a landmark, business, or intersection.

In the place card, click **Create Route** before entering the destination in the **To field**. Another option would be to click the **Swap Directions** button before entering the starting point in the From field. If need be, you could also click **Directions**, then alter the starting and ending locations. After that, click **Plan**. Select **Leave** or **Arrive** to choose when you want to leave your starting point or reach your destination. To enter a new date, you can select it from the calendar or click the date to enter a new one.

Time is of the essence when you want to plan a route. Therefore, you should also click the time you intend to leave or arrive. If you are driving, you can click **Options**, then **Choose** to avoid highways and tolls if you wish. When taking public transportation, you can choose which transit options you desire to use, be it bus or ferry. In the toolbar, click the **Share** button and choose the device you wish to send directions to. You will receive a notification on your device. To open directions in Maps, tap the notification.

7.2.1 Sending Directions To Your iPad, Apple Watch, Or iPhone

If you are signed in with your Apple ID on both your Mac and your other device, you can send a location or directions to other devices. In the Maps app on your Mac, click a location on the map. Before making any adjustments that you would like to, click **Directions**. Go to the toolbar and click the **Share** button. Select the device that you want to send directions to. After these steps, you will get a notification on your device. To open the directions, tap the Maps app on your device.

7.3 Create Reminders

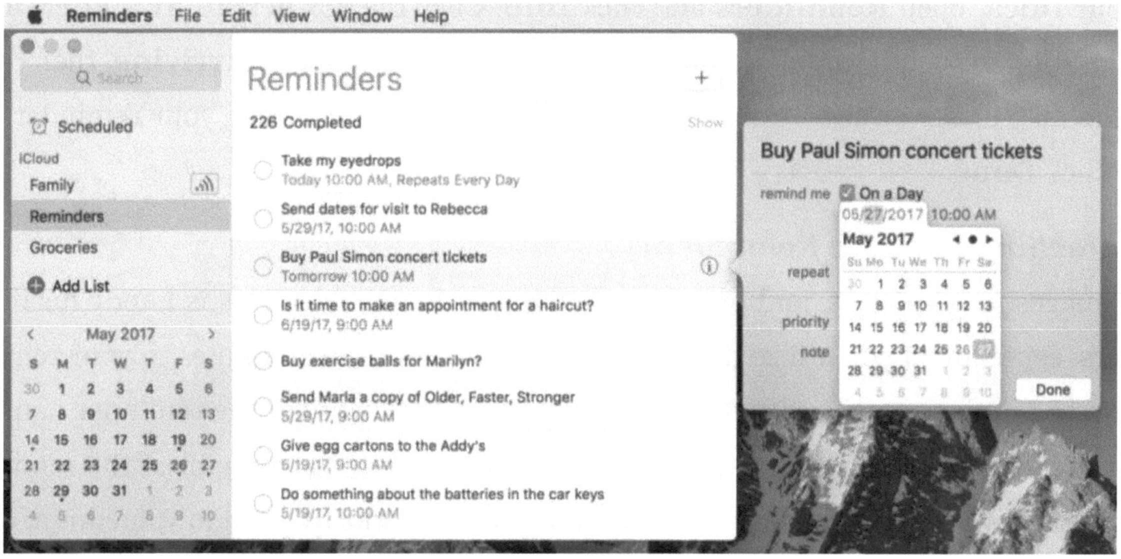

If you want to stay on top of your tasks, start using Reminders on Mac. With this application, you can track your most important tasks. Keep your to-dos in sync on all your Apple devices through iCloud.

7.3.1 Adding A Reminders Account Provider

From your **Dock**, open and click **Reminders** in the Menu bar. Afterward, click **Add Account** and choose the type you want—for example, iCloud. Click continue and enter your account credentials. Click **Sign In** and check the box that is next to **Reminders**. Select the apps that your account should be used. Finally, click on **Add Account**.

To create a reminder, go to your dock and open **Reminders**. Click the + button and write out your reminder. If you want to schedule a due date for a reminder, click **Reminders**, then the **Info** button. The Info option looks like an 'i' and it appears when you hover your cursor over the reminder. Click the **On a Day** option before entering the date for your reminder. After entering the date, enter the time for your reminder, then click **Done**.

7.3.2 Setting Up Recurring Reminders

To set up a recurring reminder on your Mac, select the task you want to set up the recurring reminder for. Under **Item Details**, go to **Reminders** and select it. Upon selecting the Reminders option, a small window will pop up. On that small window, select the **Repeat** option and you will see a drop-down menu. From the drop-down menu, choose the option you wish to set for recurring reminders, then select it. Take note that you can choose to set your reminder on an hourly, daily, weekly, monthly, or yearly basis. When you follow these steps, your recurring reminders will be set.

7.3.3 Setting Up A Location Notification For A Reminder

From your **Dock**, open **Reminders** and click **Info**. Click the box next to **At a Location** and enter a location for your reminder. You can choose either **Leaving** or **Arriving**, then drag the dot on the map closer or away from the pin to set the location in which your reminder should trigger. Click **Done**.

7.3.4 Attaching Items To Reminders

Adding images, notes, URLs, and priority to reminders is possible. This is handy for different reminders, especially if you utilize the app for school or work. To add notes to your reminders, click **Info** at the right of the reminder. Afterward, click **Notes** under the reminder name, then type in your notes. You can select your priority by clicking Info at the right of the reminder. A drop-down box will appear, from which you can choose the priority, be it low, medium, or high. For attaching images, click **Info** at the right of the reminder. After that, click the **Add Image** option for you to attach the photo.

7.4 Create And Sharing Notes

It is possible to write notes and change the formatting in a note. For instance, you could change the alignment, font size, or write in bold text. When you start typing a new note, you could apply paragraph styles if you use notes stored on your Mac or upgraded iCloud notes.

7.4.1 Customizing The Notes Toolbar

Like the other Mac apps, Notes contains a customizable toolbar at the top. This is handy when creating a new note, inserting media, adding a table or checklist, and changing your view. To change the buttons in the toolbar, right-click in the toolbar area, then select **Customize Toolbar**. Alternatively, from the menu bar, click **View** and choose **Customize Toolbar**. After that, drag buttons from the bottom options into the toolbar, where you wish them to be. It is also possible to arrange the buttons in the order you prefer. When you finish, go ahead and click **Done**. You will notice that a button or two may disappear from the toolbar. This is probably due to the window size. If the window is not wide enough to accommodate all the buttons you choose, look for the arrow to the right of the Search box. Click that arrow to see your other buttons.

7.4.2 *Writing A New Note*

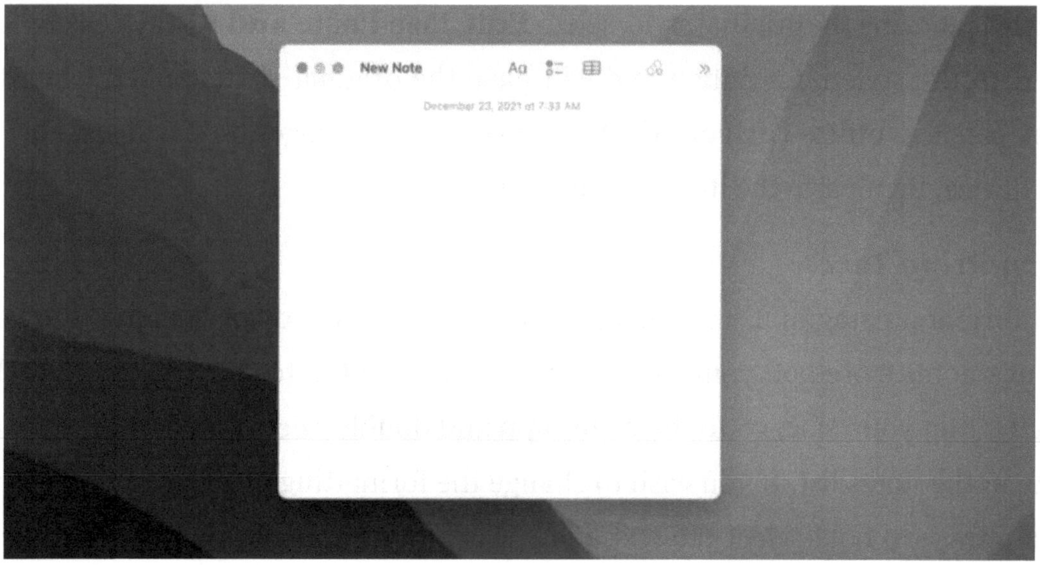

On your Mac, go to the sidebar in the Notes app and click the folder where you want to put the note. If you do not see the sidebar, click **View**, then **Show Folders**. Click the **New Note** option in the toolbar and type your note. If available, you can use typing suggestions. The first line of the note serves as the note's title. You can change the first line's formatting in **Notes preferences**. Please note that as you work, your note is automatically saved.

7.4.3 *Editing A Note*

To edit a note on your Mac, go to the Notes app and click a note in the notes list. You could also double-click a note in the gallery view. To quickly find the Notes app, you could also search for notes. In the note text, click where you want to edit or select the text you wish to alter, then make your alterations.

7.4.4 *Creating A Copy Of A Note*

In the Notes app on your Mac, click an unlocked note. Afterward, choose **File**, then **Duplicate Note**. Alternatively, you could press **Command** and **D** on your keyboard.

7.4.5 *Copying And Pasting Text*

In the Notes app on your Mac, double-click a note in a gallery view or click a note in the notes list. To copy all the text in a note, start by selecting all the text. Click anywhere in the note text, then choose **Edit** before clicking on **Select All**. An alternative way of highlighting all the text is to use the keyboard shortcut of pressing **Command** and **A**. After highlighting all the text, choose **Edit**, then **Copy**. Alternatively, press **Command** and **C**. To paste text, select **Edit**, then **Paste**, or press **Command** and **V**. When you paste, some formatting is retained, while the original color and font may not be retained.

To paste text using the surrounding style, select **Edit,** then **Paste and Match Style**. When you want to paste text using the original style, select **Edit**, then **Paste and Retain Style**. The copied text stays with the style information and will have the original style applied when the text is pasted. You can also utilize **Universal Clipboard** to copy images, text, videos, and photos on one Apple device, then paste the items on another.

7.4.6 Formatting Text

To quickly format a paragraph, you can apply a style such as body or heading. Remember that you must use notes stored on your Mac or upgraded iCloud notes for paragraph styles. When formatting text on your Mac, go to the Notes app and double-click a note in the gallery view or click a note in the notes list. If you wish to change the formatting of selected text—for example, changing a phrase to bold-select the text and click the **Format** button. Afterward, choose the desired option. To change the text alignment, click anywhere you wish to change in the text. Choose **Format**, then **Text**, before choosing the option you want.

To change the text size, color, and font, to change the text you wish to change. Control-click the selection, select **Font**, then **Show Fonts**. After that, make the changes using the **Fonts window**. If you want to apply a style to a paragraph, click anywhere in the text you want to format. The next step is to click the **Format** button, then select a style. To change the default title paragraph style, select **Notes**, then **Preferences**, you will see a pop-up menu from which you should click **New notes** to start with. Afterward, choose an option.

7.4.7 Sharing Your Notes

You may want to share notes on different applications or with other people. This helps you to efficiently collaborate in the best manner for you. Suppose you have a specific note you want another person to edit or view; follow the next steps. From the toolbar, click **Add People**. Alternatively, from the menu bar, click **File**, then **Add People To**. Choose the name of your note. From here, it is important to choose the method you prefer to share the note with that person, be it Messages, AirDrop, or Mail. Next to **Permission**, select either **Only people you invite can view** or **Only people you invite can make changes**. If applicable, complete the **Add** field, then click **Share** before following the prompts to invite a friend to look at your note.

7.4.7.1 Using Your Share Menu

To share your notes, you could use the Mac Share Menu extensions. In the toolbar, click **Share** or **File**, then **Share**. Select the service or app, then follow on-screen instructions to share or send your note.

7.5 Pick A Call

Imagine a situation where your iPhone is ringing, you need to answer the call, but you are just too lazy to go and get it. With a feature called iPhone Cellular calls, you can answer that call using a nearby Mac or iPad. The feature is part of Apple's Continuity system, which is built on sharing and syncing certain capabilities across iPadOS, iOS, Mac, and the Apple Watch.

To use this feature, your iPad must have at least iOS 8 or iPadOS, while your iPhone must be running on iOS 8.1 or later and activated with a carrier. The operating system for your Mac must be OS X Yosemite or later. If you have a Mac Pro or Mac Mini, it must also possess an external headset or microphone to utilize this feature.

As mentioned earlier, each device must be signed in to FaceTime and iCloud with the same Apple ID. In addition, they must be Wi-Fi enabled and connected to the same network, be it Ethernet or Wi-Fi.

7.5.1 Answering Or Declining Calls On Your Mac

When a call notification appears in the top-right corner of the screen on your Mac, you can accept an incoming call by clicking **Accept**. If the person calling you has set up Real-Time Text (RTT) for the call and you prefer to answer it that way, click **RTT**. If you want to decline a call, click **Decline**. If the call has come from someone you are not comfortable receiving calls from, but you can block the caller.

In some cases, you may not be able to answer a call but you can respond by sending a message to the caller. To decline a call and respond by sending a message using iMessage, click next to **Decline**, before choosing. After that, type your message, then click send. You must both be signed in to iMessage for this communication to work. At times, you may want to decline a call and set a reminder to call back later. In this case, click next to **Decline** and select the amount of time you prefer to wait before you receive a reminder. You will get a notification when the time comes. Click it to view the reminder. Afterward, click the link in the reminder so that you can start the call. If your Mac has a Touch Bar, you can easily use it to accept, decline, decline and set a reminder, or decline and send a message.

Chapter 8:

Popular Apps

8.1 Calendar

The Calendar ensures that appointments are never missed. Create multiple calendars and manage them from a single location to keep track of your busy schedule.

Create occasions. Double-click + anywhere on the calendar to add a new event. To invite someone to an event, double-click the event, then click the Add Invitees section and enter their email address. The calendar notifies you of invitation responses.

When you add a location to an event, the calendar displays a map, estimated travel time and departure time, as well as the weather forecast.

A calendar for all aspects of life: Create distinct, color-coded calendars, for example, for home, work, and school. To create a new calendar, select File > New Calendar, then Control-click each calendar to change its color.

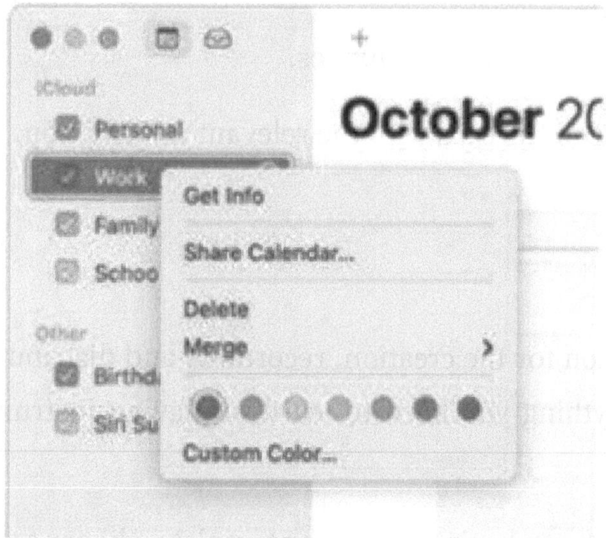

View all of your Calendars or a select few. To view a list of your calendars, click the Calendars button; then, click the calendars you wish to view in the window.

Share information between your devices and with others. When you are signed in to iCloud, your calendars are synchronized across all of your Macintosh computers, iOS devices, iPadOS devices, and Apple Watches that share the same Apple ID. Sharing calendars with other iCloud users is also possible.

8.2 Contacts

The Contacts App is the main repository on your Mac for everyone you know including their phone numbers, email addresses, and even social media information. With MacOS, you can also start a call or text, someone right from a contact's card.

8.2.1 How To Add A New Contact

If you like to add your contacts manually, or if you get new contacts you like to add, you can input them straight into the app.

1. Open Contacts on your dock.

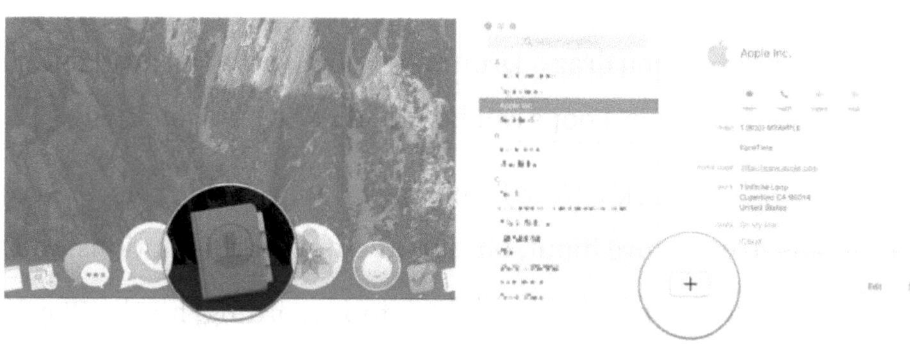

2. Click the + button at the bottom of the current contact card.

3. Click new Contact.
4. Enter the contact's first and last names.
5. Fill out the fields on the card with the relevant information.
6. Click done.

8.3 Garage Band

GarageBand is an application for the creation, recording, and distribution of music. Your home recording studio has everything you need to learn to play an instrument, compose music, or record a song.

Create a new project. You can begin with a song template, choose a tempo, key, and additional options, then click Record and begin playing. Construct your song using different tracks and loops, for instance. Click Quick Help and hover over items to learn their names and how they function.

Bring the beat in. Using Drummer Loops, you can quickly incorporate drums into a project. Click the Loop Browser , then drag a Drummer Loop to an available Tracks area. Using a simple set of controls, Drummer Loops can be modified to suit your song.

Record your voice. Select Track > New Track, then under Audio, select microphone. Click the triangle beside Details to configure input, output, and monitoring options, then click Create. To begin recording, hit the Record button, and to stop recording, hit the Play button .

8.4 iMovie

iMovie enables you to transform your home videos into stunning movies and Hollywood-style trailers that you can easily share.

Import a video. Import video from your iPad, iPhone, or iPod touch, as well as from a camera or existing media files on your Mac. iMovie generates a new library and event.

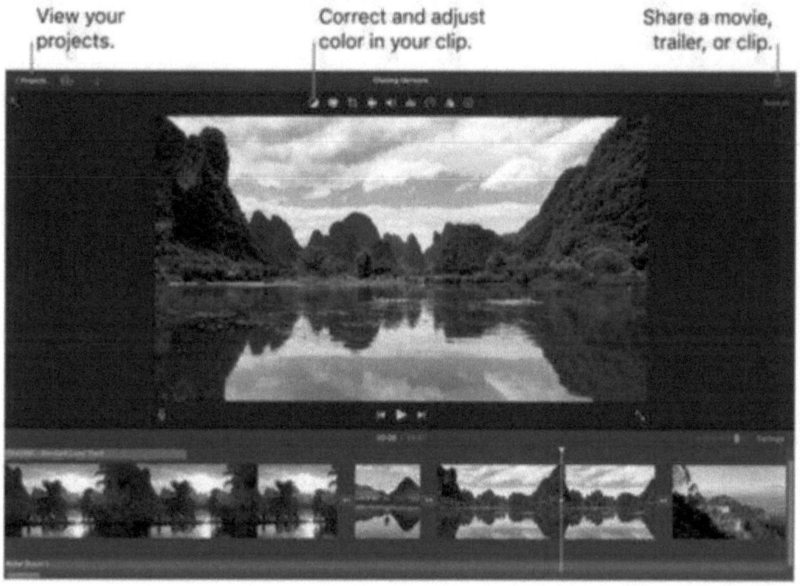

The built-in camera can record video. Record video using the FaceTime HD camera on your Mac and incorporate it into your project. To begin and stop recording, select an event in the sidebar, click Import in the toolbar, select FaceTime HD Camera, and then click the Record button.

Create trailers in the style of Hollywood. Create intelligent trailers with animated graphics and soaring music. Simply add photos and videos and personalize the credits. To begin, click the New button +, then click Trailer, before selecting a template from the Trailer window and clicking Create. Add the cast and credits to the Outline tab, as well as your images and videos to the Storyboard tab.

Tip: Shooting video with a handheld device can result in shaky footage, but you can stabilize the footage to improve its playback. Select the clip in the timeline, then click Stabilization, followed by Stabilize Shaky Video.

8.5 Keynote

Keynote allows users to create professional, cutting-edge presentations. Start with one of the over 30 predesigned themes and customize it by adding text, new objects, and modifying the color scheme.

Organize graphically. Utilize the slide navigator on the left to add, rearrange, and delete slides quickly. Select a slide and press Delete to delete it.

Practice leads to mastery: To practice your presentation, select the Play > Rehearse Slideshow menu option. You will see each slide alongside your notes and a timer to help you stay on schedule.

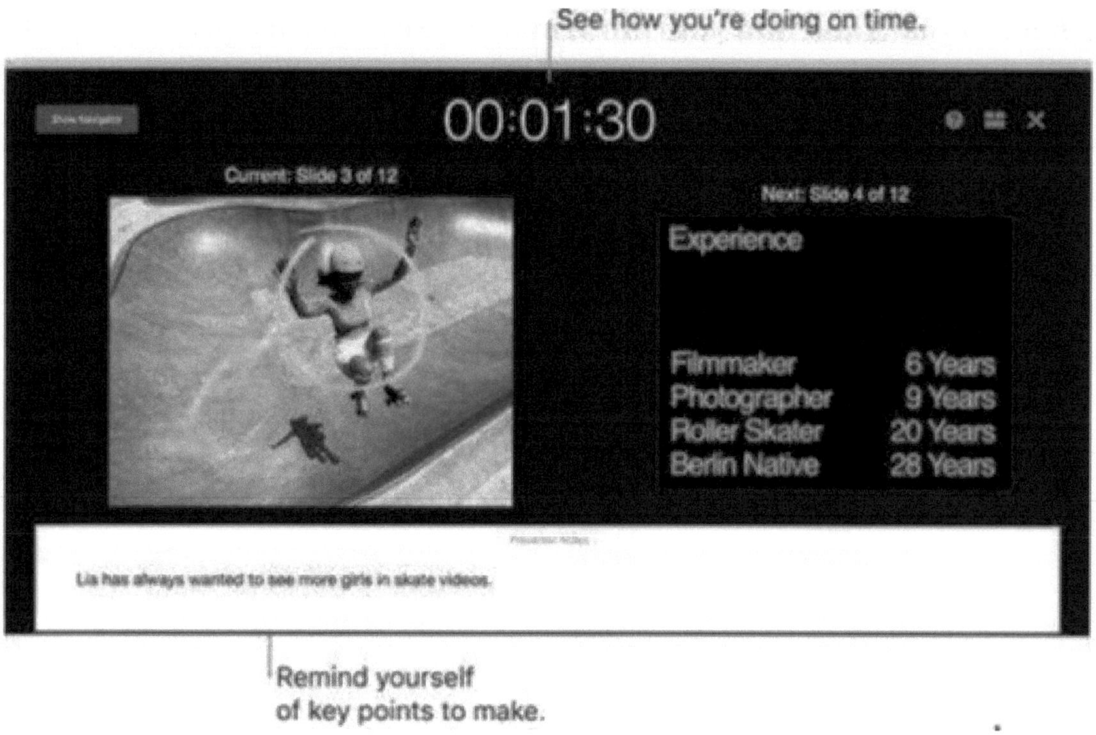

Present in all circumstances. Present using an external display while using your Mac to view upcoming slides, presenter notes, a clock, and a timer. Control a multi-presenter slideshow during a videoconference as you WOULD if you were the only presenter. Create an interactive presentation that is controlled by the audience, control your presentation remotely with your iPhone, iPad, or even Apple Watch, and more.

Share your presentation with others. If your manager wants to review your presentation or you want to share it on a conference call, select Share > Send a Copy to send a copy via Mail, Messages, AirDrop, or social media.

Draw in: Get their attention by animating a slide's object. Select the object, then click Animate in the toolbar, Action in the sidebar, and Add Effect.

You may incorporate a video into your presentation. Click the desired location, then click the Media icon  in the toolbar. Click Movies, then locate the desired video and drag it to the slide.

8.6 Numbers

Use Numbers on your Mac to create attractive and powerful spreadsheets. More than thirty templates designed by Apple give you a head start on creating budgets, invoices, and other documents. Microsoft Excel spreadsheets can also be opened and exported in Numbers.

Start with a template and add your information. Select the template's sample text, then enter your text. Drag a graphic file from your Mac onto the placeholder image to add images.

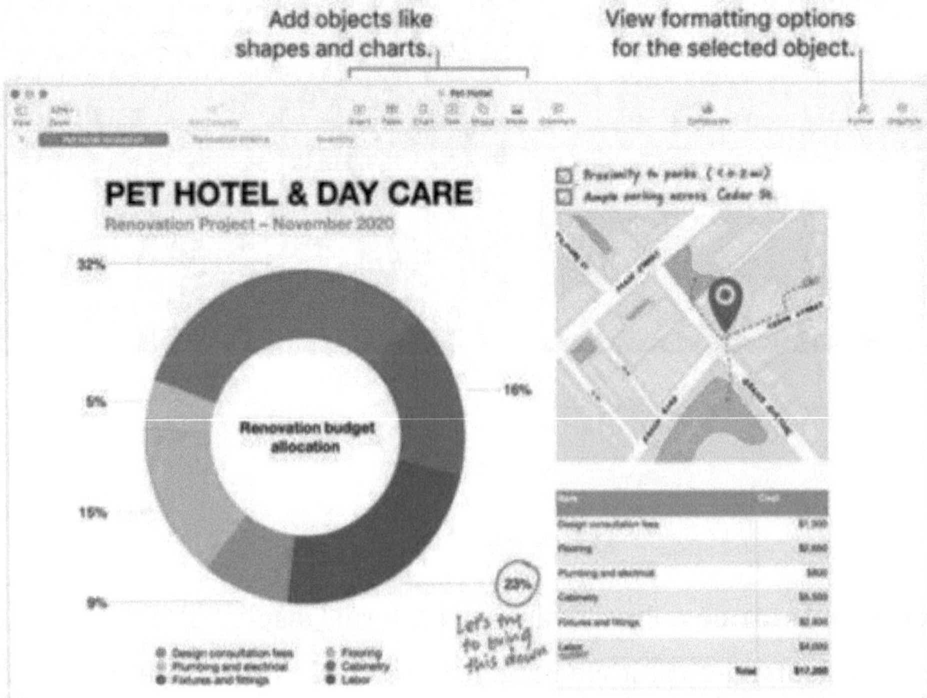

Use sheets to organize yourself. Use multiple sheets or tabs to display a variety of data views. Use one sheet for your budget, another for your table, and a third for your notes, for instance. Simply click to add a new sheet. To rearrange sheets, drag a tab to the left or right.

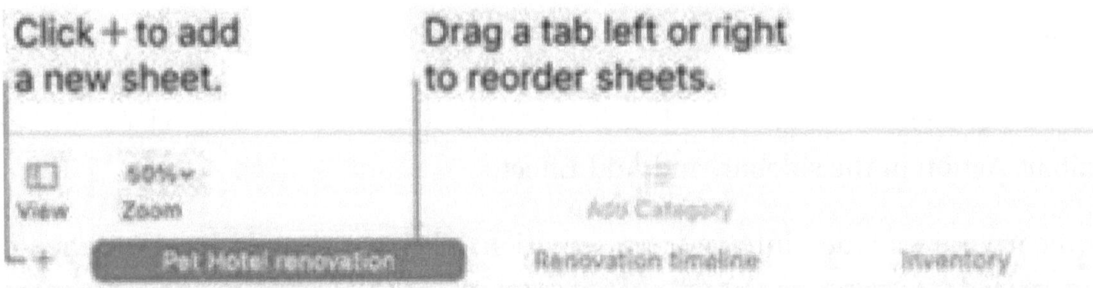

Formulas are trivial. Simply type the equal sign (=) in a cell to view a sidebar with a list of all the functions and their descriptions. When you begin to type a formula, instant suggestions will appear.

Select the range of cells containing the values to receive instant calculations for a series of values. You'll find the sum, average, minimum, maximum, and count of the selected values at the bottom of the window. To view additional options, click the Menu button in the bottom-right corner.

Build pivot tables Create a pivot table using a table or range of cells in a spreadsheet as the source data, and then use it to analyze any data set, quickly group and summarize values, and identify interesting patterns and trends. You can modify the cell range of your source data, add and organize pivot table data, and create a copyable snapshot of a pivot table.

8.7 Pages

Create media-rich documents and books on your Mac using the Pages application. Open and edit Microsoft Word documents while keeping track of changes made by yourself and others.

Look good! Pages provide professional, ready-to-use templates for books, newsletters, reports, and resumes, making it simple to begin a project.

All formatting tools in one location: To open the Format inspector, select the Format button in the toolbar. When you select an item in your document, the formatting options for it will appear.

The text must flow around images. When an image is added to a text document, the text will automatically flow around it. In the Format sidebar, you can adjust the wrapping of text.

Move a graphic into a text block... **...and the text wraps around the graphic automatically.**

Develop publishing skills. Pages include book templates for creating EPUB-formatted interactive books. Include both text and images, as well as a table of contents. When ready, you can make your book available in Apple Books for purchase or download.

Start on the Mac and finish on the iPad: When you sign in with the same Apple ID on all of your devices, you can keep your documents up to date. So you can begin writing on one device and continue on another.

Rapidly translate. Select the text you wish to translate, Control-click it, select Translate, and then select a language. Click "Replace with Translation" to translate typed text. Additionally, you can download languages for offline use by navigating to the Language & Region section of System Preferences and clicking the Translation Languages button at the bottom.

Tip: Enable change tracking to view the modifications you and others have made to a document. Each individual's edits and comments are color-coded, allowing you to determine who made each change. Select Edit > Track Changes to display the tracking toolbar.

8.8 Voice Memos

Voice Memos make it simpler than ever to record personal reminders, classroom lectures, interviews, and even song ideas. With iCloud, you can access the iPhone-recorded voice memos directly on your MacBook pro.

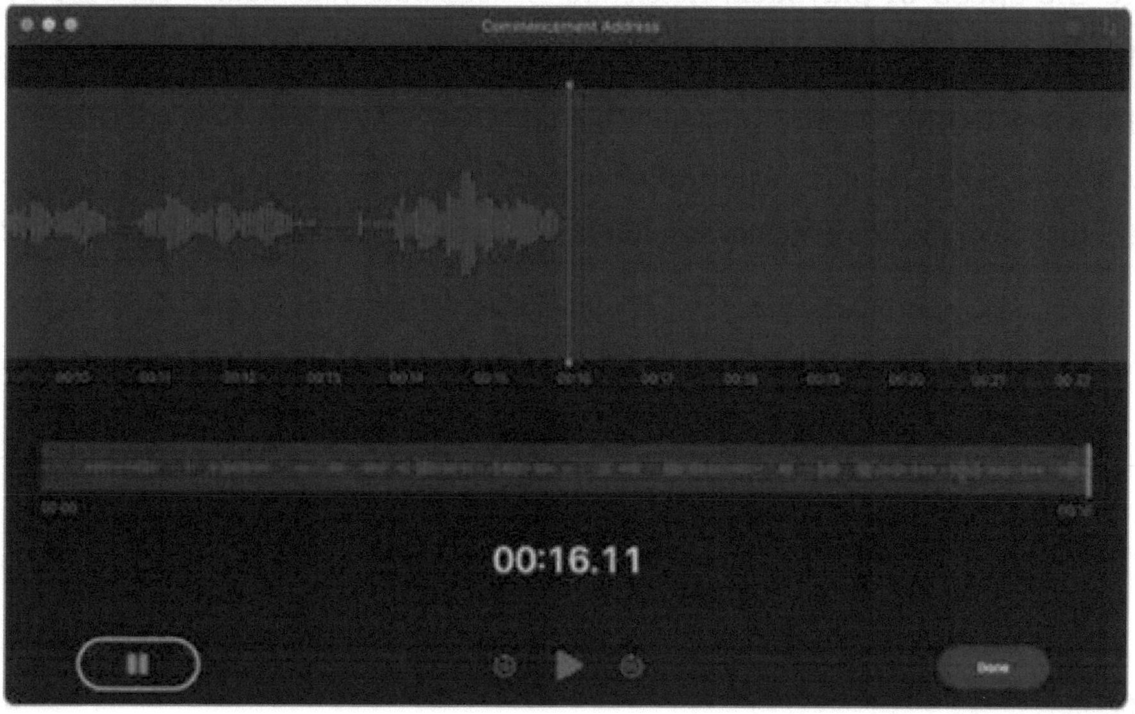

You can record on your MacBook pro. To begin recording, click the Record button, and to stop, click the Done button. A recording can be renamed to make it easier to identify. Click the default name and then enter your own. To listen to your recording, press the Play button.

Your voice memos across all your devices: When you sign in with the same Apple ID, your voice memos are accessible on all your devices. You can access iPhone or iPad-created recordings directly from your Mac.

Use folders for an organization: Create folders to help you organize your Voice Memos. Click the Sidebar button, then click the New Folder button at the bottom of the sidebar to add a folder. Enter a folder's name, then click Save. To add a recording to the folder, hold Option while dragging the recording into the folder.

Make an audio recording of a favorite. Select a recording, and then click the Favorite button in the toolbar to easily locate the recording in the future. To view your favorite items, click the Sidebar button.

Skip silence. Bypass pauses in the audio. Select Skip Silence by clicking the Playback Settings button at the top of the Voice Memos window.

Change the speed of playback. Accelerate or decelerate your audio. Click the Playback Settings button atop the Voice Memos window, then drag the slider to the left or right.

Amplify a recording. Reduce ambient noise and room reverberation to enhance the audio quality of your Voice Memos. Activate Enhance Recording by clicking the Playback Settings button at the top of the Voice Memos window and selecting Enhance Recording.

Chapter 9:

Security And Antivirus

9.1 Updating Your Mac's Operating System And Applications Is Important!

In order to keep your Mac secure from hackers, it's best to maintain your Mac's software and apps up to date. Because they know where to look for security flaws that developers only fix in newer versions, cybercriminals target out-of-date software.

Updating your macOS software to the most recent version of OS X is a simple process. To update your Mac, just click the Apple symbol at the top of your screen, pick About This Mac > Software Update, and follow the on-screen directions to complete the process.

It's possible to arrange for future OS X updates to be installed automatically after you've installed the most recent version of macOS on your computer. Automatically keeping my Mac up to date may be found in the System Preferences under Software Update.

It's also simple to keep all of your applications and apps up to current. Make sure that the Automatically check for updates and the Install app updates checkboxes are checked in your System Preferences under the App Store heading.

9.2 Get Rid Of Your Computer's Default Security And Privacy Settings

Default settings on your Mac may allow Apple and other programs to share and access your data, such as use data and location, as well as other information.

The following are some of the details included within:

- Passwords for devices.
- Access to your contacts, calendars, and other private information is granted to the app.
- Services that help you find your way about.
- Sharing of diagnostic and use data.

To begin, go to System Preferences > Security & Privacy. Set a password for your Mac and disable automatic logins under General. You can also modify the time it takes for a password to be required when your Mac goes into sleep mode. One of the safest (and simplest) methods to protect your data is by using a strong device password.

Additionally, there are a few privacy settings that must be addressed. To view all the applications that have access to your data, including your location, contacts and calendars, go to the Privacy tab.

By deselecting the proper options under Diagnostics & Use, you'll notice if you're unintentionally transmitting usage data to Apple, as well. Uncheck the programs you don't want to have access to your data, and then decide whether or not Apple should get an automatic report of your Mac's usage.

9.3 Use A Browser That Protects Your Privacy

It might be tough to keep yourself and your personal information safe while exploring the internet. If you're concerned about your online safety and privacy, you may want to use a browser other than Safari, which is incorporated into Apple's operating system.

Google Chrome and other popular browsers aren't going to secure your privacy.

One of the greatest methods to keep yourself safe online is to use a secure browser. Brave, Opera, and Tor are all examples of safe browsers.

To protect your privacy, these browsers include built-in measures to ensure websites aren't tracking your browsing activities or your IP address, which is used to determine your actual location. Scripts embedded in scam websites that might infiltrate your device are likewise blocked by Brave's browser.

9.4 Antivirus Software For Macs Is Essential (That Actually Works)

There are various antivirus programs available, but many of them do not adequately guard against macOS-specific malware, especially in light of the fact that hackers are increasingly turning their attention to Macs and developing sophisticated threats against them.

Security protections incorporated into Apple's operating system are not sufficient to protect your Mac from ransomware, spyware, and keyloggers.

- An increasing number of phishing assaults are taking place.
- Breach of personal information.
- Macs may be protected from ransomware and internet assaults by antivirus programs like Intego and Airo AV.

9.4.1 The Importance of An Antivirus

Although it is true that Mac computers are more secure than Windows systems, these Apple devices must have added protection through the use of antiviruses. The vulnerability of Macs to viruses and other malware is a quickly developing problem. In 2021, a study revealed that in 2020 alone, there had been a 1000 percent increase in the level of malicious programs that target Mac computers. In addition to the built-in security system of Apple devices that remarkably keeps malware at bay, you need to tighten your protection by installing antivirus software.

There are plenty of options when it comes to installing antivirus software on your Mac. Some of the ones that you can install include Norton, Intego, AVG, Kaspersky, and Bitdefender. Let's get more information on each of these antivirus software's.

9.4.1.1 Norton

To find the Norton antivirus software, visit www.Norton.com. This option is one of the best on the market. Norton has a 360 Deluxe AV tool. With this software, you qualify to be offered a first-year discount. The software has been reduced from a price of $104.99 and currently costs $39.99. Included in the Norton package are services that include VPN coverage, parental controls, and PC cloud backup. Furthermore, you can use it on five devices.

9.4.1.2 Intego

The antivirus software called Intego Mac Internet Security X9 is a friendly solution for the wallet. Its yearly price has been reduced from $84.99 to $39.99. This software was particularly built for Macs. In addition to other features that it offers, it possesses a location-based firewall and provides protection from phishing scams. You will find Intego on www.intego.com.

9.4.1.3 AVG

For simple virus protection, you can choose AVG's free tier. It allows you to scan for infected files on your Mac. The free tier also ensures that your new downloads are free of the virus payload. There is also an upgrade to the free tier. The paid AVG tier includes phishing and ransomware protection. In addition to that, it has a Wi-Fi inspector, which functions to monitor all the devices that are connected to your home network.

9.4.1.4 Kaspersky

To find Kaspersky Internet Security for Mac, visit www.Kaspersky.com. Kaspersky usually has good scores in independent tests. From a price of $79.99, this software's price has been reduced to $39.99 for an entire year's protection. Kaspersky has webcam spying protection and a content filter that is used for parental control.

9.4.1.5 Bitdefender

Visit www.Bitdefender.com to access the Bitdefender Antivirus for Mac. This inexpensive option of protection has a number of features. It costs $29.99 for a whole year of protection from malware. Bitdefender Antivirus for Mac has an autopilot feature, in addition to a built-in Virtual Private Network.

9.5 Keep Your Passwords Safe With A Password Manager

What steps are you taking to protect the security of all of your account passwords? Using a strong password to lock your Mac is a must, as previously said. Nevertheless, what about when you're going into your social media accounts or online banking portals?

- Using a password manager is a good idea for a variety of reasons, including:
- Keep your passwords in a safe place.
- Instantly generating fresh passwords with a high level of security.
- Logging into websites and applications faster.
- For online buying, storing credit card information.

iCloud Keychain, Apple's proprietary password manager, is available. You may use it to keep track of your passwords, usernames, and credit card details. AES 256-bit encryption, sometimes known as "military-grade encryption," is used to encrypt all data.

Because it can only be used with Apple products like Safari, iCloud Keychain is only of limited utility. You won't be able to utilize it to log into websites if you use a different browser.

If your credentials are exposed in a data breach, this password manager will not alert you. Additionally, you won't be able to update all of your passwords at once, so you'll have to do it one at a time.

9.6 A Two-Factor Authentication System For Icloud

As an example, a random one-time code (OTC) is required when connecting to your accounts using two-factor authentication (2FA).

Even if a hacker has your passwords, they will be unable to access your data using two-factor authentication because of the randomly created one-time password.

You should implement two-factor authentication (2FA) on all of your online accounts, but you should start with iCloud.

9.7 iCloud Two-Factor Authentication: Here's How To Do It

Users of Mac OS Catalina: Select Apple ID > Password & Security from the System Preferences menu. Create a Two-Factor Authentication System.

- For Mac OS: Find two-factor authentication under the System Preferences iCloud section and click on the button that says "Set up Two-Factor Authentication."
- The two-factor authentication codes will be sent to your phone number.
- A one-time password will be sent to your iCloud account every time you log in on a new device or log in online from now on.

9.8 Protect Your Data Using Encryption

Basically, encrypting your files implies encrypting your data with a password to protect it. In this way, a thief or hacker won't be able to gain access to your private data or crucial documents stored on your device.

FileVault Apple's built-in encryption tool makes it simple to protect your most private data.

Chapter 10:

System Preferences

10.1 Users And Groups

This chapter discusses how to create extra user accounts on your Mac for each individual to personalize their own settings and preferences without affecting others.

Create a New User Profile

1. Select Apple Menu> System Settings.

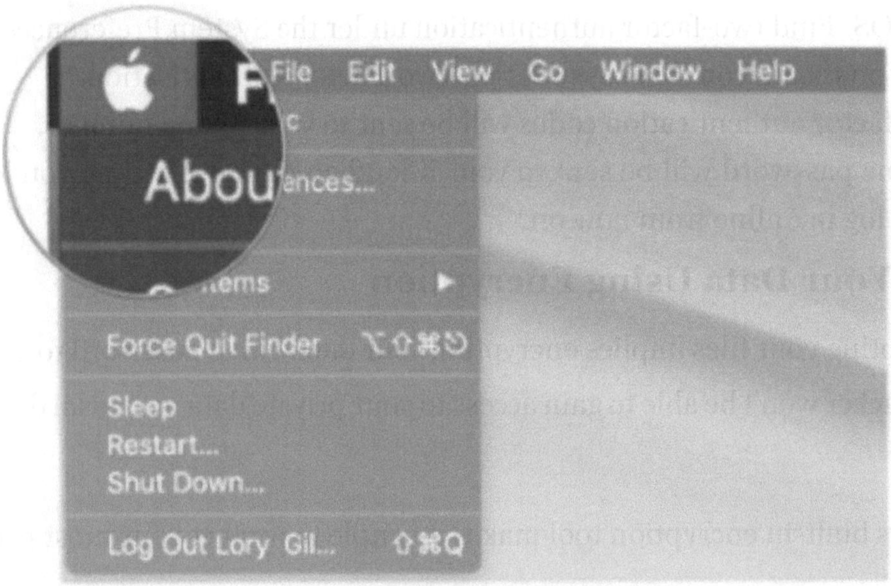

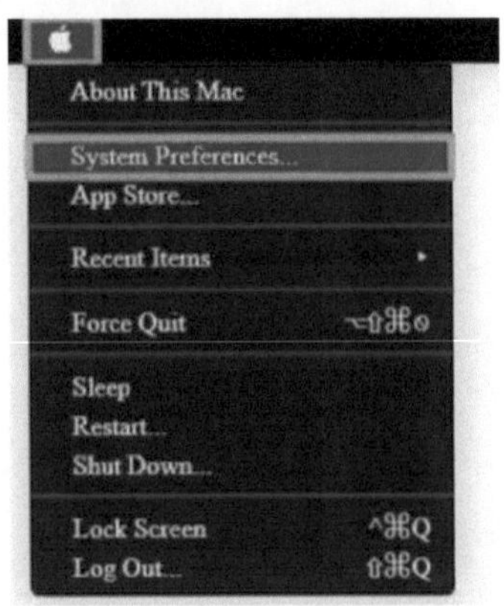

2. Select users and groups. 

3. Select the lock icon in the corner to open users and groups.

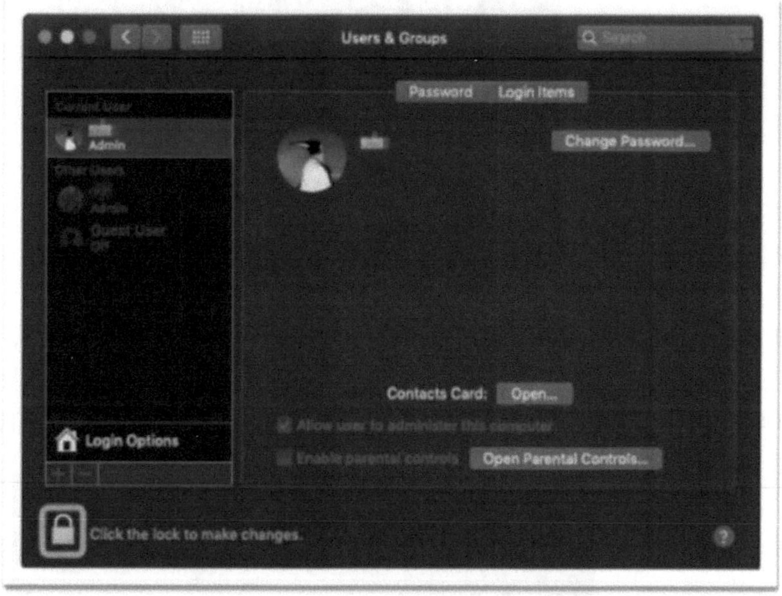

4. Enter your password and select Unlock.

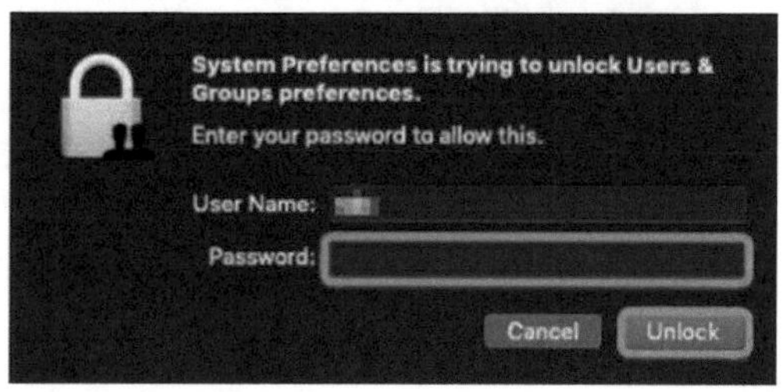

5. Select the  Icon on the bottom left to create a new account.

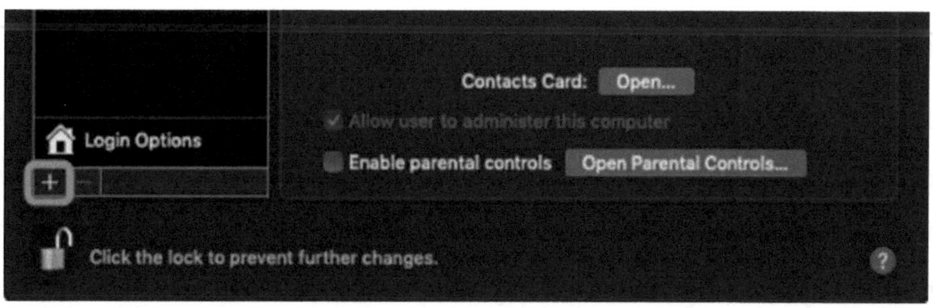

6. A new account is opened. At the top, select the type of account you want to create.

7. If you are creating a managed parental control account, select the age range of the child.

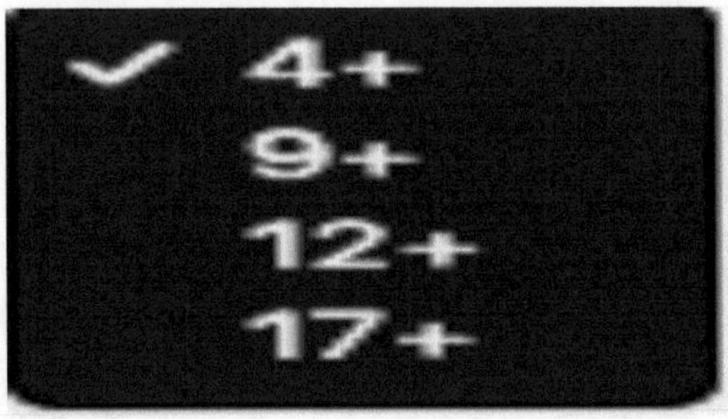

8. For all user types, enter a username, account name, and password, and enter it twice.

You can also enter a password hint to let the user know if they forgot their password.

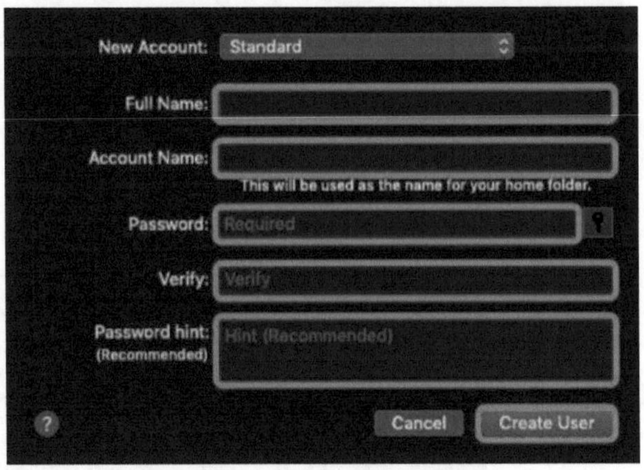

9. Select Create User.

10. You will see that your new user appears in the list on the left.

10.2 Family Sharing

Family sharing is an important tool that allows a maximum of six people to share content, be it Apple Books, iTunes, Fitness+ subscriptions, or Apple Music Apple Plan. You can also share family calendars, locations, and photo albums. Interestingly, all this is done without sharing accounts. The Family sharing functionality works across Macs and iOS devices. In this section, you will learn how to set up family sharing on your Mac.

10.2.1 Setting-Up Family Sharing On Mac

The first step is to open **System Preferences**. This could be through your **Dock** or the **Apple** menu. Click on **Family Sharing**, which you will find at the top right side of the System Preference window. You will be required to confirm your Apple ID. After that, you will get prompts for inviting family members.

10.2.2 Adding Family Members

It is not mandatory that you add all the members of your family the moment you set up Family Sharing. It is possible to add them as you go and as you deem fit. You can even remove members if you choose to. Please note that you can only add up to a maximum of five family members.

Adding people to Family Sharing on a Mac involves going to **System Preferences** prior to clicking **Family Sharing**. Don't forget to select **Family** in the sidebar that is on the left side of your screen. Click **Add Family Member** and you're done. Each family member that you add to Family Sharing will receive an iMessage that serves as an invite to the Family. The invited family members have the leverage to accept or deny being part of Family sharing. They have to tap on the iMessage and agree to join. Only then will Family Sharing work for them.

10.2.3 Selecting Features To Share

Considering that there are many things that can be shared through Family Sharing, it is less likely that you want to share all of them. For this reason, you should select the features that are going to be shared with your family members. Here are some of the options that are available:

- **iCloud Storage:** This allows you to share your iCloud storage with members of your family. Let's say you have a storage plan that allocates you two terabytes of storage space, and you can share this with your family members.
- **TV channels:** Suppose you subscribe to a Premium streaming service like Apple TV+. You can let your family also enjoy it without having to pay anything extra.
- **Screen Time:** Monitoring the screen time of a child in the family can become much easier. All you have to do is create a Child Account, set screen limits, and also view reports.
- **Purchase Sharing:** You can share any other media that you buy, except for in-app purchases. Examples of media that you can share include Books and iTunes.
- **Apple arcade:** You can even share Apple's gaming subscription service with the members of your family. They won't have to pay anything for them to access the service.
- **Location sharing:** It is possible for you and your family members to share your locations or those of your devices. However, please note this functionality is only available for people in the Find My app, which is a tool that helps to find the location of your device.

Having discussed some of the options that you may consider as you share features with your family, there are a few things that we need to clarify. These relate to some of the features that you may possibly share.

- **iCloud:** Some might fear that if they share iCloud storage with their family members, their data will be exposed. This is not the case. People sharing iCloud storage cannot see the information that is stored by other people they are sharing their storage space with.

You only share the amount of data in numbers, but your storage spaces are completely separate.

- **Purchase sharing:** The moment you enable purchase sharing, the members of your family will access iTunes features, Books, and most of the apps that you purchase at the App Store. However, they will not access app subscriptions and in-app purchases. The moment you enable Purchase Sharing, anything involving purchases are charged to the Organizer of your family. This still applies even if the family member buys features that cannot be shared and the Organizer still has to pay.
- **Apple TV and Apple Music Channels:** When you share these channels, your content and playlists still remain private to yourself. In the same way, you cannot see the playlists of other family members too. When each of you accesses Apple Music or Apple TV, each of you has their separate recommendations and play history, just as it would be if they were paying their subscriptions on their own.

10.3 Restrict Contents

It's good that gadgets like the Mac make it easy for kids to access information that is relevant to them. Such important information includes content that is related to their academic learning objectives. However, the internet can be a very unsafe environment for your grandkids if they access content that is toxic to them, like pornography. Thank goodness Mac has functionalities that help you protect the hidden in your family from such harm. You can restrict content that can be streamed on a minor's account. The goal of this section is to discuss how you can restrict content on a MacBook.

10.3.1 Creating A New User Account On Mac

Usually, people have only one user account on Mac, which is also known as the administrator's account. If that is the case with you, then you should create another account for the minor in your home. For most seniors, this could be a grandchild or probably the youngest child. To create this separate account for the child, go to **System Preferences** through your Dock. Among the options you see, select **Users and Groups**. At the bottom left side of the screen, you will see a **lock**, be sure to tap on it. The next step would be to unlock your accounts and this requires you to enter the username and password of the administrator's account. Go to the bottom left side of the screen and tap on the + that is there.

Switch the **type of account**, putting forward **Standard** as your choice. You will then be required to enter the **full name** of the child you are opening the account for. Also, create a **password** for that account and **verify** it in response to prompts on your screen. Creating a password hint is a great idea, just in case you forget it. As the last step, click **Create User** and a new account will be created. If there are more children staying with you, use the same procedure to create their own accounts too.

10.3.2 Turning On Screen Time On MacOS

Now that the kids have their accounts, you don't want them to spend all their time staring at the screens. You can activate settings that give the kids restrictions as far as screen time is concerned. The first step in achieving that is turning on the screen time. If you have never done it before, you are at the right place.

Open **System Preferences** and click **Screen Time**. Normally, the administrator account is selected by default. However, just check to make sure that it is selected. Go to the **Options** button that is located at the bottom left screen region and click it. At the top right side, click **Turn On**.

10.3.3 Setting Restrictions On All Devices

Screen Time has another function that allows you to put in place restrictions for all the devices in your home that children use. So, you set restrictions on one device, and the other devices pick up the same restriction. However, this does not just happen, the devices should be set to do so. Let's delve into the nitty-gritty of how you can set your devices accordingly.

Through **System Preferences**, go to **Screen Time**. Again, just check if the administrator account is selected, it should always be by default. Click the **Options** button prior to checking the box that is adjacent to **Share across devices**. You're all set!

10.3.4 Adding A Passcode To Screen Time

Advances in technology have gone to stages where children can easily navigate through devices and even customize settings to their own preferences. You wouldn't want that to happen in Screen Time because then the children can alter the restrictions that you would have put on them. You, therefore, need to add a passcode in a bid to avoid such a scenario.

Adding a passcode begins by selecting **Screen Time**, having entered **System Preferences**. Toggle the **child's account** and then click **Options**. Identify the **Use Screen Time Passcode box** and check it. Enter a passcode with four digits and then re-enter it as the prompts on the screen direct you.

10.3.5 Using Screen Time For Downtime Scheduling

Downtime refers to that moment where the other apps do not work on the child's account, except for the ones that you choose to allow. This comes in handy if there are certain apps that you want the child to focus on. They will have no option to use the apps that are working in their account at that given time. Downtime also works when there are some apps that are not bad for your child or grandchild, but you want to control the amount of time that the child spends on them.

To schedule Downtime for macOS, click **System Preferences** and then **Screen Time**. Toggle the child's account and then click **Downtime**. You will have to activate Downtime by clicking the **Turn-on** button. Decide on the schedule that you would like to set and then choose **Custom** or **Every Day**. When you select Every Day, Downtime will take place each day at the same time. When you choose Custom, there is more flexibility involved. You can change the time for Downtime every other day. You can even turn off Downtime on some days if need be. Interestingly, there is also an option for completely blocking the child's account during Downtime. To do this, simply choose **Block at Downtime**.

10.3.6 Setting Time Limits For Apps

At times when you don't want to restrict the use of some apps, you can limit the amount of time your child uses them. So, in this case, you want the child to use the apps, but not for too long. Screen Time also has such functionalities.

To start, open **Screen Time** in **System Preferences**. After toggling the **child's account**, click on **App Limits**. You will find the latter on the left side of the screen. Activate the time limits by clicking **Turn on**. Now, it's time to add the app category. Do so by clicking on the + symbol. Next to each app category is a check box. **Check** the one that is adjacent to the app category that you want to limit. Click on the Expand **icon** so that you can see the apps that are being affected by your selection. Highlight the app category before setting the time limit to your preference. Select either the **Every Day** or **Custom** schedule to determine the recurrence of the time limits. If there are other app categories that you would like to limit, follow the same procedure as described in this section. When all app categories of choice have been given time limits, click **Done**.

In the event that you then want to remove the time limits that you set, go back to **Screen Time** and toggle the **child's account**. Click on **App Limits** and then uncheck each of the app categories whose time limits you want to drop. Click **Turn Off** in the event that you want to stop app tracking.

10.3.7 Setting Always Allowed Content

Depending on your assessment, there might be other content that you never look forward to restricting from the children. Such content is what we refer to as "always allowed." To set this up, open **Screen Time**, toggle the **child's account** and then click on **Always Allowed**. Go on and check the boxes that are adjacent to the time that you want the child to always access without limitation.

10.4 Monitor Settings

You can customize monitor settings on your MacBook. This contributes to creating an environment that you enjoy or, rather, that suits you. For instance, it is possible to alter settings such as brightness to match your preferences. If you have problems with your eyesight, you should avoid looking at too bright screens, especially for extended periods of time. In this section, the main focus is on giving you ideas on how you can adjust monitor settings. Let's dive in!

10.4.1 *Adjusting Brightness*

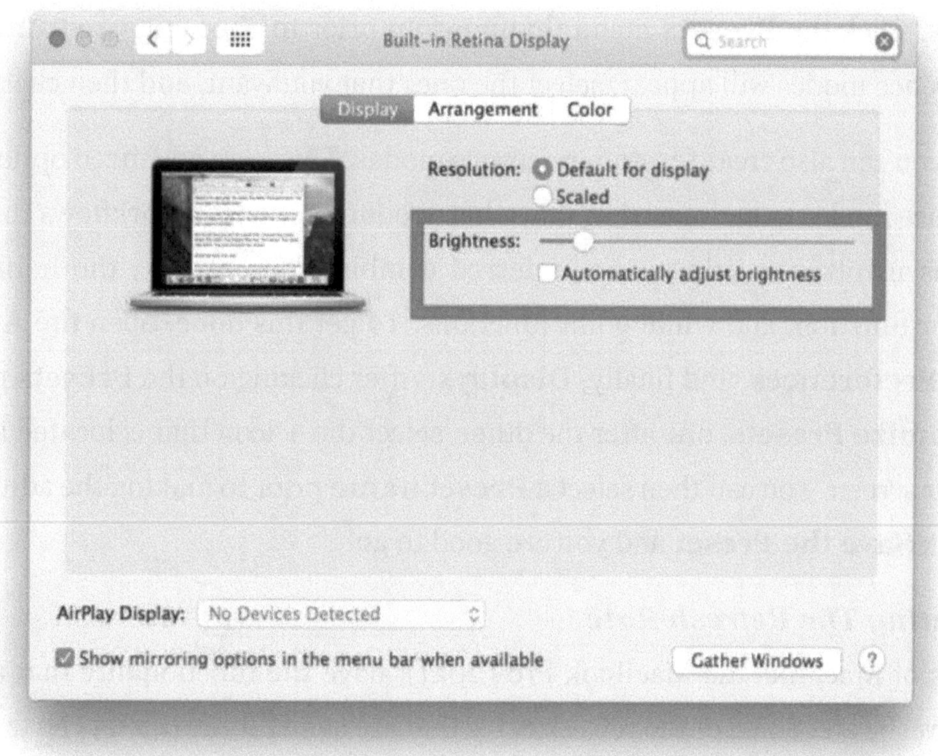

Adjusting the brightness on your Mac begins by clicking on the **Apple menu**. This menu is available on the top left corner of your screen. Go to **System Preferences** and select **Displays**. In some cases, you will find a slider that you can move to and fro to adjust the brightness on the screen of your Mac. Sometimes, you simply have to check or uncheck on **Automatically adjust brightness**, depending on what is best for you. For example, if you're comfortable with the device-determined brightness settings that your computer will set for you, check **Automatically adjust brightness**. Special brightness requirements are best met when you make the adjustments manually.

10.4.2 Altering Reference Modes

Reference modes help to set characteristics of various media types, including SD, HD, and HDR videos. They set the white space, brightness, color space, and gamma on the display of the media types. As such, you can alter the reference modes to match your preferences.

If you want to adjust the reference modes, open the **Apple Menu**, go to **System Preferences**, and then choose **Displays**. A **Presets** pop-up menu will appear; click it to select the reference mode that you want to adjust. An alternative method for adjusting reference modes is by going to the **Menu bar** and then clicking on the **Airplay** menu. Click **Reference Modes**.

Now you know how to adjust reference modes, but do you know how to choose the ones that are dear to you? To choose a reference mode, go to the **Apple menu**, **System Preferences**, and then **Displays**. Click the **Presets** menu that pops up prior to choosing **Customize Presets**. Different reference modes will appear, select the ones that you want, and then click **Done**.

Interestingly, you can also create custom reference modes. This is an advanced option that allows custom reference modes to be weaved in ways that produce enhanced workflows that are unique in nature. This involves creating your preferred combinations of, say, the luminance, color gamut, transfer function, and white point functions. To get this done, open the **Apple menu**, then **System Preferences**, and finally, **Displays**. After clicking on the **Presets** pop-up menu and the **Customize Presets**, one after the other, select the + icon that is located at the bottom left side of your screen. You can then select a **Preset name** prior to making the adjustments that you want. Click **Save the Preset** and you are good to go!

10.4.3 Adjusting The Refresh Rate

Some versions of Mac, like the MacBook Pro (2021), have the functionality that allows you to change the refresh rate. Some of the refresh rates that are available are 47.95 Hertz, 48 Hertz, 50 Hertz, 59.94 Hertz, and 60 Hertz. The moment you make the decision to change the refresh rates, here is the number one tip: select the refresh rate that can be evenly divided into your content's frame rates. This means that the refresh rate that you will choose is highly dependent on the frame rate of your content. For instance, if your content's frame rate is 25 frames per second, the 50 Hertz refresh rate might be appropriate.

To start adjusting the refresh rate, open **Displays** by choosing the **Apple menu** and then **System Preferences** in their order of mention. When the Refresh Rates pop-up menu appears, click on it. Select the refresh rate that you want and make sure it is appropriate with regard to the frame rate of your content.

10.5 Changing Resolution

Altering the resolution on your MacBook is not as complicated as you might think. Go to the **Apple menu**, click **System Preferences**, and then select **Displays**. In the event that the Resolution is set to Default with regard to display, click **Scaled**. To the left of **Default**, there are boxes that you can click on if you want to enlarge the text. Would you prefer more space on the screen so as to accommodate many things? If yes, simply click one of the boxes that are located at the right of **Default**.

10.6 MacOS Updates

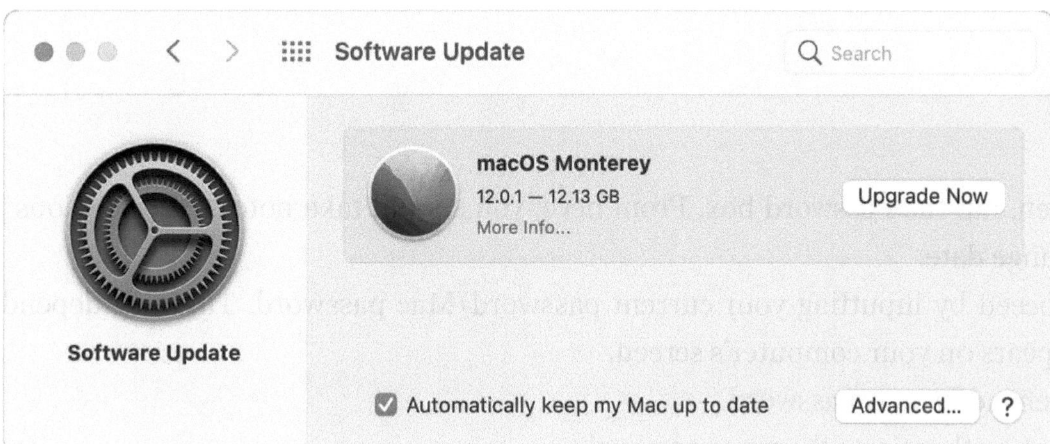

Just like your smartphones and other computer devices, your MacBook Pro requires an update from time to time; this is to avoid bugs, crashes, as well as viruses.

- Tap the Apple icon at the upper-left of your MacBook Pro.
- From there, tap **System Preferences**. Alternately, select **About This Mac**.

- Regardless of the option you choose, tap on **Software Update** from the resulting menu.
- Hold on for your computer to connect to the internet and search for updates. If your Mac finds an available update, the Update Now option will become active. Click on it.
- To enable automatic updates, tick the "**Automatically keep my Mac up to date**" button. So, whenever new updates are available, you won't have to go through the process above; rather, you'll be automatically prompted by your Mac to make the update.

10.7 Manage User's Passwords

If you feel you need to change your Apple ID password as well as security credentials on your MacBook Pro, then you can do so freely.

10.7.1.1 Adjust Apple ID Password

- From your MacBook Pro, tap the Apple icon in the upper-left corner.
- **Next, tap** System Preferences.
- From there, tap **Apple ID**.
- From the left side of the new pane, tap **Password & Security**.

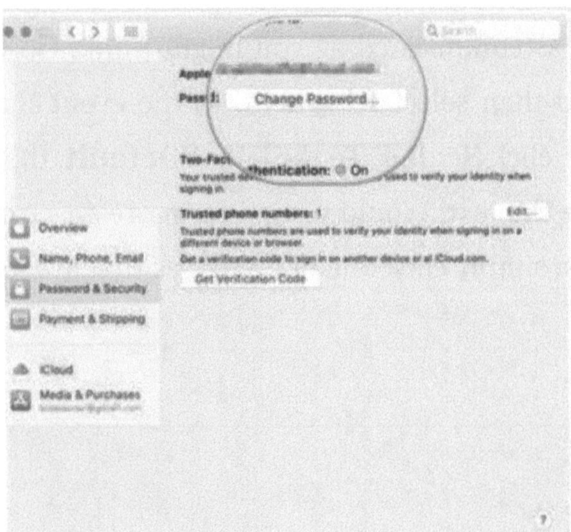

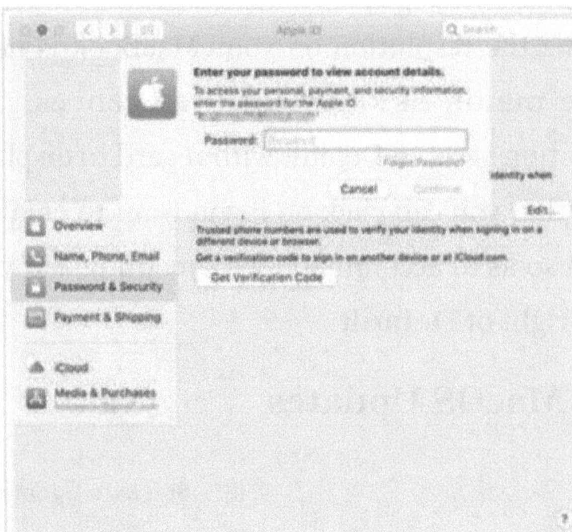

- Then, tap the Password box. From here, you should take note of the previous password change date.
- Proceed by inputting your current password/Mac password. This will depend on what appears on your computer's screen.
- Then, add a new password.
- Next, authenticate the new password.
- Now, tap **Change**.

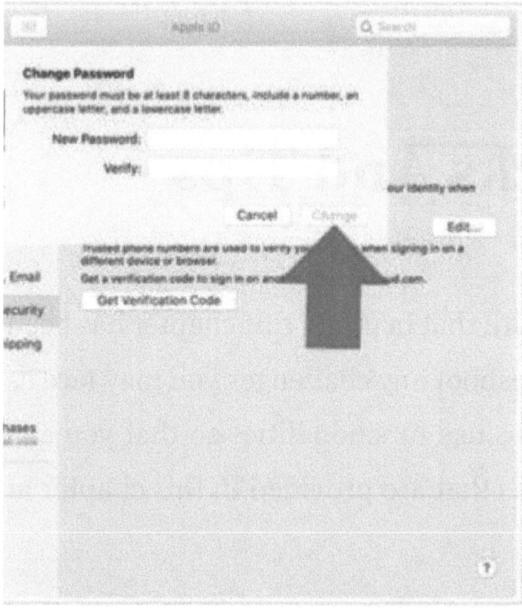

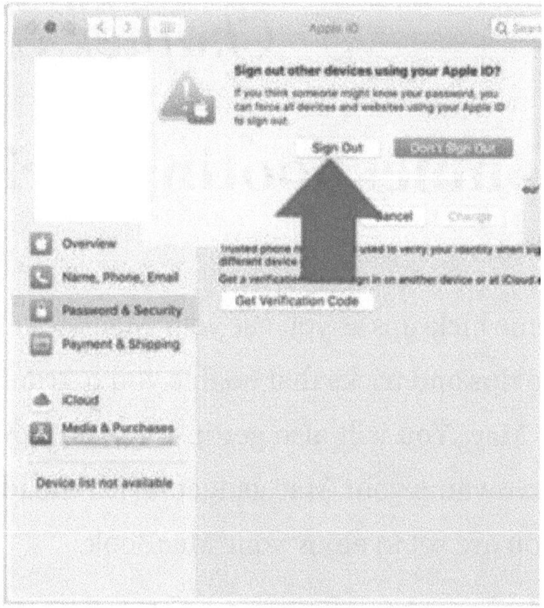

- Proceed by choosing **Sign Out** or **Don't Sign Out**. If you choose the first option, all devices and web pages associated with your Apple ID will be logged out.
- That's it! You've finally adjusted your Apple ID password. However, you'd be asked to sign in to your account once more on your other Apple devices.
- You can modify your trusted phone number and generate a verification code from the Apple ID settings on your computer if you have Two-Factor Authentication.

Chapter 11:

Troubleshooting, Tricks And Tips

You might face some hick-ups as you use your MacBook. With that in mind, this chapter has been created to provide tips and tricks that enable you to troubleshoot any challenges you may face as you operate your Mac. You will also get insights on how to use functionalities so that you can benefit more from owning your Mac gadget. With the ideas that are provided in this chapter at your fingertips, you are set to enjoy your MacBook.

11.1 Reclaim Space

Do you feel like there are a lot of things that are taking up space in your Mac? This is very normal, considering the more you use your device, the more you are likely to save documents, pictures, music, and videos. Usually, not everything that you save in your gadget remains relevant in the long run. You might need to find out some strategies for freeing up the space that is taken by the things that you keep loading into your computer. This chapter makes this goal quite easy to achieve because it gives you ideas on how you can reclaim some space on your MacBook. Choose what works for you from the strategies outlined in this section.

11.1.1 Delete Files And Apps

Take some time to review your computer and search for the content you can delete manually. See if you have files, apps, or items that are no longer relevant so you can trash them. You can also look for duplicate files that take your space unnecessarily. For instance, you might be one of those who tend to take multiple photos that look alike. Removing some of the photos and keeping one or two representatives of each set of similar photos might leave you with extra space on your MacBook.

Deleting files or apps is pretty easy. Simply right-click the name of the file or the icon of the app that you want to eliminate. Click **Move to Trash** and you are done. Please note that trashing your files and apps like this will not free space on your Mac. It's like moving the files and apps from one part of the computer to another. To successfully create more space on your gadget, you also need to go into the trash and further delete the items completely. Make a right-click on the **trash icon**, before clicking **Empty Trash**. This action will add kilobytes, megabytes, or gigabytes to your computer's free space.

11.1.2 Create ZIP Files

If you have large files that take up much space but you don't want to delete them, creating ZIP files is a viable option. ZIP files make it possible for you to compress them so that they will take less space than they would if they had remained individual files.

To create a ZIP file on your MacBook, follow these steps:

1. Identify the files that you want to ZIP. If these files are in a folder, open it first.
2. Hold down the **Command** or **Shift** keys while you click on the files you intend to add to your ZIP file. These files will appear highlighted.
3. Make a **right-click** on the highlighted files. Alternatively, you can click **File** on the menu bar positioned at the screen's top.
4. Either way, click **Compress X Items**, where X denotes the number of files you highlighted to add to a ZIP file.

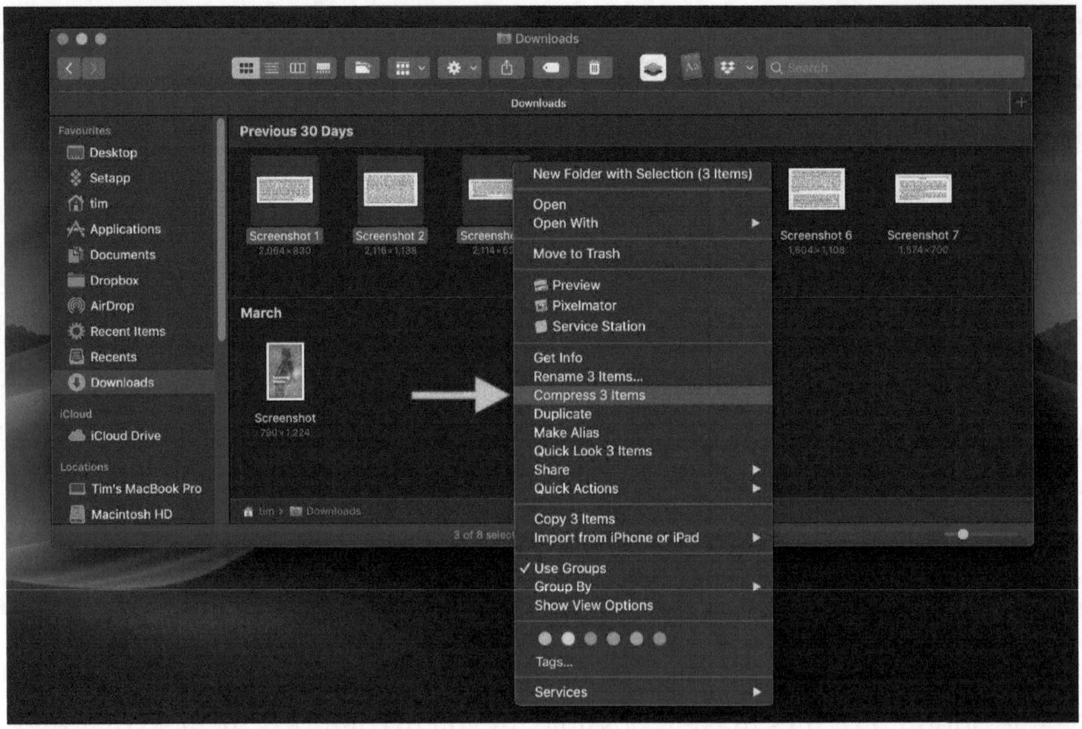

Upon completing the compression, the new file will be named Archive.zip. This file will be located in the same folder from which you took the compressed items. It's possible to change the compressed file's name for easier identification. Before selecting **Open**, you can access the files in the ZIP folder any time by just right-clicking on it.

11.1.3 Unpack Your Downloads Folder

Quite often, the downloads folder is filled with files that were once important but not anymore. Mind you, some files even get downloaded without your consent. If you go through this folder, you might be surprised to see videos, restaurant menus, memos, and work presentations that are no longer necessary. Clear your downloads folder often to create more free space on your computer.

To remove unwanted files in the downloads folder, start by clicking the **Go Tab** in Finder. To open the downloads folder, click **Downloads**. Make right clicks on each of the folders you want to remove before clicking **Move to Trash**. One more tip, make accessing the Downloads folder easy by creating a shortcut to it in your Dock. You can do this by dragging the Downloads folder from Finder to Dock.

11.1.4 Remove Temporary Files

Temporary files accumulate as you continue to use your computer. These files occupy some of the space on the hard drive of your Mac, and more importantly, you don't need them. Therefore, clearing them off your computer can free up a lot of space. Be sure to do this often to keep them off, considering that they continue to build up as you use your Mac.

Now, how do you remove temporary files? First, go to Finder and click on the tab **Go**. Second, click on **Go to Folder** and then type in **~/Library/Caches**. Click **Go** again. After this last action, you will find yourself in a caches folder. Highlight the files that you intend to delete and then make right-click on them. Select **Move to Trash**. Be sure to then remove these files from your Mac's trash bin as well. If you do not want to remove the temporary files manually, you can use the app called CleanMyMac. When you engage this app, it will not only locate the temporary files for you but also delete them.

11.1.5 Use The Storage Functionality Of Icloud

Instead of storing your files directly on your Mac, you can load them to iCloud. With Apple's storage service, you can still access your files with ease. More importantly, for this section, you will save huge amounts of space on your MacBook. If you are an Apple user, you are automatically assigned 5 GB of storage on iCloud for free. If you need more space, there is an option to buy more iCloud storage at a monthly fee. The prices are quite affordable. For instance, you can get 50 GB of iCloud storage at a fee of $0.99 per month. There are three possible options for storing files on iCloud. These options are clearly outlined below:

- **Documents and Desktop:** All files that can occupy these folders can be stored on iCloud. In cases where the storage capacity on your Mac is low, all the other files are stored on iCloud, except for the ones that would have been recently opened. To identify the files that are stored on iCloud, check for a cloud that has an arrow pointing downwards, which is the icon for iCloud. When you want to access files that are stored in iCloud, simply click on the icon and download them.
- **Messages:** Messages and attachments are also stored well on iCloud. You will only find the recently opened attachments and messages on your Mac, especially when the computer is low on storage.
- **Photos:** Photos and videos are stored in their original form with full resolution. In the event that you have little space on your Mac, only the version of videos and photos that save space can be found on your computer. However, you can still get the original versions on iCloud by clicking the icon and downloading.

To store the files on your MacBook on iCloud, go to the top-left corner of your screen and click on the **Apple icon** that is located there. Go on to select **About this Mac**. Click the following in their sequence: **Storage tab**, **Manage**, and then **Store in iCloud**. A pop-up menu will appear with the options of the types of files that you can store on iCloud, as we described earlier. Select the ones that you want and then click **Store in iCloud**.

11.1.6 Take Out Language Files

Some of the apps that are found on your Mac come with language files associated with them. This functionality is available to accommodate different languages. However, it is more likely that you will use one language among the many that are available. Deleting the language files that you don't use or need will actually free up some space on your laptop. Apps like Monolingual and CleanMyMac can delete unwanted language files for you. With Monolingual, you can get back hundreds of megabytes that would have been taken up by macOS language resources.

11.2 Back-Up Your Files

Backing up your files is one of the tricks that you will certainly need if you don't want to lose your data. You cannot overlook mishaps that affect your computer it can even die on you. If anything should happen to your computer, you should remain at peace because your data is safe. In this section, we will look at different ways through which you can keep your data safe and accessible.

11.2.1 *Take Advantage Of The Time Machine*

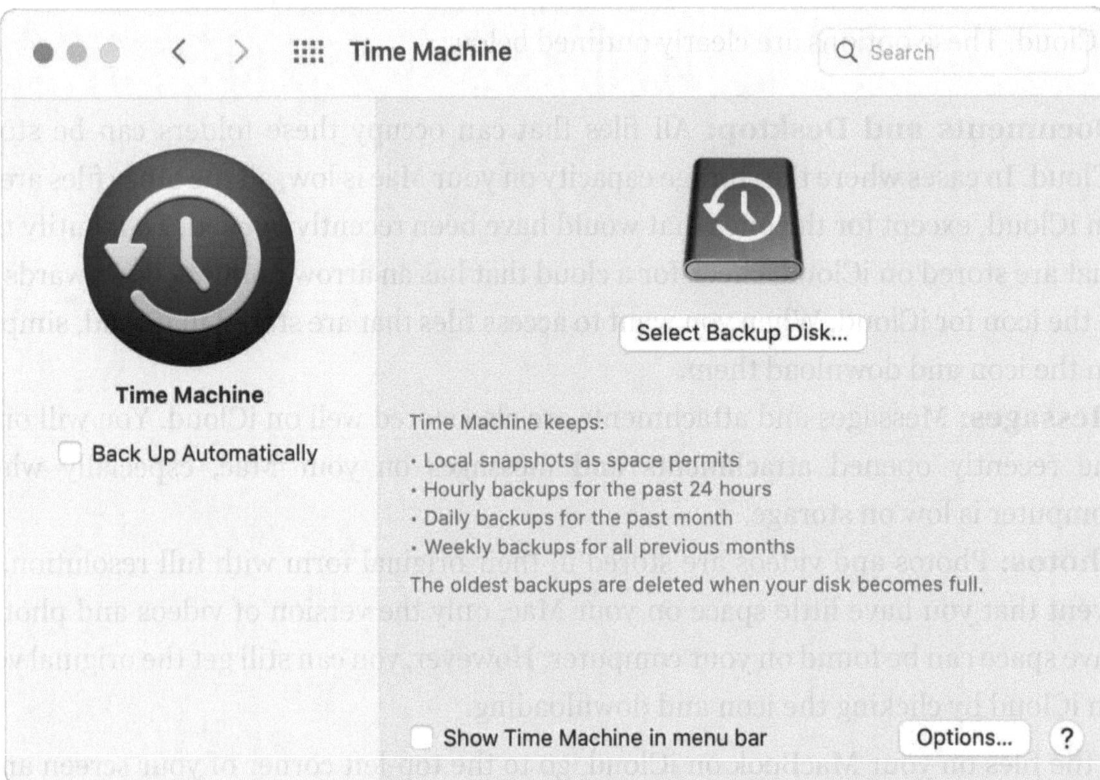

The Time Machine is Apple's own backup software that is part of the macOS. To use the Time Machine for backing up your files, plug in an external storage device: USB, SSD, or hard drive. A NAS drive that will connect to your Mac through a WI-FI network will also work.

Here is the procedure that you can follow for you to set up Time Machine on your Mac:

1. Ensure that external storage is connected to your MacBook.

2. The external storage should be formatted as Mac OS Extended. If the formatting is correct, be on the lookout for an alert on your Mac inquiring whether you would want to use the connected drive with Time Machine. Go on and click **Use as a Backup Disk**.

3. In the event that the alert does not appear, open **System Preferences** and go to **Time Machine Preferences**. Here, select **Backup Disk** before choosing the storage device of your choice. Now, click **Use Disk**.

4. You can encrypt your backup if you choose to. If you encrypt your backups, be sure to keep your password handy because it will become a requirement before you can access your files.

One thing that you will also need to remember when you use the Time Machine is to plug the external hard drive into your computer. Otherwise, no backup will be happening.

11.2.2 Use A Backup Software That'll Clone Your Mac's Hard Drive

This backup software will duplicate the information that is on the hard drive of your computer. Carbon Copy Cloner, Acronis, SuperDuper, and ChronoSync are good examples of such cloning software. As is the case with the Time Machine, you need to plug in your hard drive before you can use cloning software.

The step-by-step guide on how to clone your MacBook highly depends on the type of software that you choose. However, the procedure for all the software won't deviate much from the following steps:

1. Start by connecting your external storage to your Mac.

2. If there is a need for you to format the drive prior to use, open **Disk Utility**. Select the **external drive**, click **Erase**, and then select **macOS Extended**. Again, click on **Erase**.

3. Now, go to the cloning software and open it.

4. If the software offers you the option to copy what is on your Mac's internal hard drive to the external storage device, click on it.

5. You might be required to confirm the request in (4) above. You will do so by entering your **password**.

6. Once the copying process is complete, click **Done**.

11.2.3 Use iCloud

You can safely back up your files using iCloud. If you pay a monthly subscription for iCloud storage, you can access more space so you can backup more files. Without a subscription, you are limited to the 5 GB that you get by virtue of being a user of Apple. Backing up your information on iCloud is a great idea, especially when you have more than one MacBook. This strategy may also come in handy when you want to access your information from, say, an iPhone.

11.2.4 Go For Google Drive Or Dropbox

If for any reason, you can't use iCloud for backing up your files, Google Drive and Dropbox are viable alternatives. Although these strategies are usually used for sharing files, especially during collaborations, you can also opt for them as backup methods. However, Dropbox and Google Drive are more appropriate for backing smaller or fewer files than the ones that iCloud can hold. You can access the files that you backup through Dropbox from any other computer.

Here is how you can use Dropbox as a backup option:

1. Sign up for a Dropbox account before you download and install the application's software.
2. Open Dropbox on your Mac.
3. On the right, click on **Upload Folder** or **Upload Files**. Identify the folder that you would like to upload and then click **Choose**. Give your Mac some time to complete the upload.
4. It's also possible to drag the folders or files from their location on your Mac to Dropbox through Finder.

11.3 Recover Files From Backup

Having transferred your files to a backup drive or software, how then would you get them back to your Mac if need be? This question will be answered in this section. Let's go!

11.3.1 Using Migration Assistant

If you used the Time Machine for backup, the migration assistant is the right tool to use when you want to recover your files. Using this tool might need you to reinstall your macOS, which you should do before you can continue. To begin, your Time Machine should be connected to your Mac. Also, ensure that the Time Machine disk is switched on. Now, go to your Mac and open **Migration Assistant**. You will find it in the **Utilities** folder, inside the **Applications folder**. You will be asked about how you prefer to transfer the files. Go for the option to transfer from a Mac, startup disk, or Time Machine backup prior to clicking **Continue**. Click **Time Machine** backup and then **Continue**. Select a backup and then click **Continue** again. Identify the information that you want to transfer and select it. To begin the transfer, click **Continue**. Please note that the length of the time that it takes for your transfer to compete varies with the size of the files.

11.4 Run First Aid From MacOS Utilities

Are you facing regular app and/or system crashes? Could it be that some of your files are becoming corrupted while some simply vanish? When you start facing these issues on your Mac, running first aid from macOS utilities might just save the day. This intervention also works when your Mac is taking far too long to start up, apart from other start-up problems. If external devices are not working as expected or you keep getting cryptic error messages, then running the first aid is the way to go. This section will enlighten you on what you need to do to run first aid from macOS Utilities.

Once you diagnose the problems, the first step that you should take is to backup all your data if you weren't doing so already. After that, you can go on and deal with the Disk Utility. It is normal to feel a bit skeptical about touching this area, but there is no need for you to fear it because it's quite an easy procedure. Follow these steps:

1. To open the Disk Utility, go to **Finder**. Click **Applications** and then select **Utilities**.
2. In the sidebar, identify the disk that is giving you challenges and select it.
3. Right at the top, click on **First Aid** and then **Run**.
4. Upon completion, check for a **dropdown menu** that shows the status of the disk. When you click on it, you will get more information about the issue at hand.

Apparently, **Disk Utility** will make efforts to repair as much damage as possible. It will let you know of the available errors that it cannot correct.

11.5 Reinstall MacOS To Solve Severe Problems

Reinstalling macOS usually sounds like an extreme intervention to problems on your Mac. However, there are severe problems that may require drastic measures for them to be solved. In this section, we will look at how you can successfully reinstall macOS on your MacBook. However, before we do that, we will explore some of the problems that might require you to reinstall macOS. You might need to reinstall macOS when

- Your machine becomes super slow in operating.
- You keep getting error messages.
- Your MacBook refuses to boot.
- Software's fail to run correctly.

11.5.1 Steps For Reinstalling MacOS

Before you start the installation process, be sure to backup all your files. Also, log out of all apps. Let's delve into the details of how you can reinstall your macOS in this section.

11.5.1.1 Boot Into The Recovery Mode

To reinstall the OS for old Macs, you would need the DVD that shipped with your Mac. This is no longer the case with the newer version of Mac, particularly those running OS X 10.7 Lion or later. For the modern Macs, the built-in recovery mode will play the role that the DVD played in old Macs. To boot your Mac, shut it down first. Hold the **Cmd + R** keys and switch on the power button again. Keep holding down these keys until the Apple logo appears. Within a few seconds, a macOS Utilities page that has a variety of options will appear.

In some instances, your computer might fail to pass the Apple logo stage by freezing. If this happens, opt for the internet recovery mode. Taking this step means that the recovery environment will now be run from the internet, not your hard drive. To start the internet Recovery mode, press **Cmd + Option + R**. This time, expect a spinning globe, not the Apple logo.

After the startup process, make sure you are connected to a Wi-Fi network. Give your Mac enough time to download the recovery environment. Select your language. Please note that the system may reinstall a version of macOS that is different from the one that you had before you used the Internet Recovery mode. For instance, you might get Lion when you initially had Mavericks.

11.5.1.2 Erase The Disk

Please note that you can skip this step if you don't want to lose any data upon reinstalling your macOS. However, if you want to follow all the steps, then you have to erase the disk. To start this process, go to the menu and click **Disk Utility**. After this, check the options on the left sidebar and choose your internal hard drive. This drive is usually labeled as Macintosh HD. On the right side, there is an **Erase tab**; click it. Check to see that the format appears as Mac OS Extended. By clicking **Erase**, you will be confirming the operation. After this procedure, it's time to reinstall your macOS, so quit the Disk Utility by holding down the **Cmd** + **Q** keys.

11.5.1.3 Reinstall MacOS

Now that you have completed clearing your information off your computer, you can reinstall your macOS. Doing this depends on how you booted your computer. Suppose you booted it from a USB disk, then you should click **Continue** and you will be taken to the installer. In the event that you booted it from a functioning recovery partition, go to the **Restore macOS** button and click it. This will trigger the installation process to begin. When you get to a point where you are asked which hard drive you would want to install your macOS onto, select the Macintosh HD because it is the one that you selected earlier on.

Please take note that the installation of macOS might take some time, so be patient and do not disturb it. Soon after the installation is complete, your Mac will restart on its own and you will be requested to create an account. Follow the prompts and enjoy improved functionalities on your Mac!

11.6 The Genius Bar To Resolve Troubleshoot

The Genius Bar is the support counter that is found at Apple store locations. The employees who work there are well trained at the corporate headquarters for Apple. They are experts in dealing with technical issues pertaining to software and hardware. Therefore, if you want assistance with troubleshooting issues on your device, the Genius Bar is the place to go. Please note that the Genius Bar does not fix problems that are associated with your cellular service. Moreover, the Genius Bar does not guarantee that the problem that you are facing with your device will be resolved all depends on the type of problem. However, in most cases, the issues are resolved.

To get services at a Genius Bar, be sure to book an appointment, and please do so ahead of time. The first step in doing this is to go to the Apple website. At the bottom of the screen, click the **Apple Retail Store** link. When the link opens, go down to the **Genius Bar** section and select **Learn more about the Genius Bar**. On the right side of the screen, find the **Genius Bar**

Reservations tab and click it. You will be prompted to choose a state and location. Upon following the prompts that appear on the screen, you will book your appointment.

Be prepared to pay for the services from the Genius Bar unless your device is still covered on a limited warranty. Please note that the warranty only works for you in this case if the issues on your device are due to bad workmanship or parts that are faulty. If the damage is due to mishandling practices or accidents like falling, you will have to pay for the services that you get at the Genius Bar.

Be sure to back up your information before you take your device to the Genius Bar because there's a chance that some of the information in your device might disappear during the troubleshooting processes, depending on the type of problem being resolved. Therefore, ensure that all your videos, music, contacts, and apps are synced through iCloud or iTunes. This way, you will have a backup copy of your valuable data.

11.7 More Tips And Tricks

At this point, you might have gained a lot of knowledge about navigating through your Mac, as well as taking care of it. In this section, you will learn more tips and tricks that will lay a great foundation for you to become an expert in dealing with your Mac. Here are some of the fascinating ideas that you will be glad to have come across:

- **Swap between desktops:** If you are using multiple desktops, switching between them is quite easy. Simply press the **Control** button and then punch the left or right arrow.
- **Copying links:** Do you want to copy links faster in Safari? Simultaneously press **Command** and **L** so that you highlight the URL bar. To copy, press **Command** and **C**.
- **Quick access to the dictionary:** Suppose you find a word that you do not understand, highlight the word and then press on it with the Force Touch Trackpad. A dictionary definition of the highlighted word will appear on your screen.
- **Sign PDF documents:** If you want to sign some documents that have been sent to you, drag the document to an email message. At the top right, you will find a button with a down arrow. Click **Markup**. Click the box that appears like a signature. Click **Trackpad** and then use the mouse to sign on to the trackpad. Alternatively, you can write your signature on a white sheet and then capture this signature using Webcam. To do this, click **Camera** to show that this is the option that you are choosing. Save the signature for recurrent use.
- **Create your own keyboard shortcut:** There are default keyboard shortcuts that you might be used to. Did you know that you can create your own keyboard box with the option for you to choose the application of choice? You will also be prompted to choose the menu

command and keyboard shortcut that you prefer. Finish off by clicking **Add** and you are all set!

- **Get invisible files in Finder:** No more troubles getting the invisible files in Finder anymore. Simply click **Cmd**, **Shift**, and the **period** (.).
- **Resizing a window:** There are many other options that you can use to resize the window, but most of them shift the proportions of the window. To avoid this problem, press **Shift** as you simultaneously resize the window from the corner or edge. When you use this method, the window is resized from the center. Interesting, isn't it?
- **Extending battery life:** There are a number of available options that can assist you in extending the battery life of your Mac. These include turning off the WiFi and Bluetooth, doing away with runaway applications, ensuring Spotlight indexing is turned off, lowering the brightness of your screen, and turning-off Time Machine. You can even select Energy Saver Preferences and keep them on.
- **Creating an auto duplicating file:** If there is a file that you want to open in duplicate, click the file, right-click, and then choose to **Get Info**. Go to the Stationary Pad Box and check it. Once you do that, the file will open a duplicate whenever you click it. This comes in handy when you are dealing with templates.
- **Hiding a window:** Hiding a window from your desktop can be quicker than you can imagine. Just press **Command** and **H** and the window will disappear. Pressing **Command** and **Tab** will bring the hidden window back.

Conclusion

As you grow older, you might have more time for yourself and your family, considering that you might have retired. Your Mac might be your best acquaintance, even though your family and friends are miles away. This device might be a tool for communication with your loved ones and assist you with access to entertainment and information. With the fast-paced technological advances, you can use your MacBook to do various things like making payments. However, you need to know how to use the device to enjoy the benefits of owning one. This book is handy because it provides a comprehensive guide on how to use and deal with your Mac.

This book starts with enlightening you on various terms you are more likely to come across as you use your Mac. These terms include software, hardware, app, browser, CPU, and Wi-Fi, to mention a few. Knowing these terms helps you understand the step-by-step guidelines outlined in this book. We also highlighted the different MacBook types, which are MacBook Air, MacBook Pro, and iMac. Please note that the MacBook Pro can be with or without a touch bar. If you have eyesight issues, the MacBook with a larger screen is a great choice, if you don't have one already.

Guidelines on how to start-up your Mac are clearly explained in this book, along with other ideas for customizing the Dock so that its appearance appeals to you. Some of the tasks you want to complete on your Mac require the internet, which is why this book taught you how to connect to Wi-Fi. Not only that, but tips on choosing the right browser were also brought forward. We zeroed into the Safari browser because it is the brainchild of Apple. All this is meant to make your experience on the internet as enjoyable as it can be.

Using your Mac for entertainment makes you more likely to navigate through different media such as music, videos, and pictures. Not to worry, this book explains how you can use these functionalities. You can even share media with others as described. Here are even more tasks that you can compete with your Mac:

- Receiving and sending emails
- Starting and receiving FaceTime calls
- Chatting through messages
- Taking selfies using Photo Booth
- Reading books
- Watching TV and movies
- Exploring the world using Maps

If you are staying with children who might also need to access your Mac, you can create accounts for them that are separate from yours. Doing this allows you to plan and monitor the type of activities that the children can become exposed to. This protects the minors from information that is possibly toxic to them. Various other security features are available on your Mac. You can access these System Preferences, which is the pane where you can customize the settings of your computer to match your needs and wants.

If you have problems with your Mac, this book provides tips for troubleshooting them. For example, if your Wi-Fi does seem to work, restarting your Mac might solve the issue. If your gadget is becoming slower when completing tasks, it might be low on space. Ideas and tips for reclaiming your space—deleting some files and apps, creating ZIP files, and getting rid of temporary files—were also highlighted.

In the case that you have been unable to solve the problems that are affecting the proper functioning of your computer, you can book an appointment with the Genius Bar that is nearest to you. At the Genius Bar, your gadget will be checked by experts who have been properly trained to do so. Please note that it is crucial for you to backup your information when you take your Mac to the Genius Bar. There are several backup strategies that you can use. You can use Time Machine, iCloud, and Dropbox as backup tools. Serious problems on your Mac might prompt you to reinstall your macOS. Again, this measure requires that you backup your data.

The book ends by giving you some tips that make your navigation through your Mac as easy and fast as possible. For instance, you can create your keyboard shortcuts, in addition to the ones that default to your Mac, like the Command plus C for copying. Did you know that just pressing the Control button while punching the left or right arrow is another way to switch between desktops? It's even much easier than the conventional way of switching from one desktop to the other. I hope that as you get to the end of this book, you will have gained a lot of insights and confidence to navigate through your Mac.

Happy MacBook Exploring!

9 781801 886475

Printed by Libri Plureos GmbH in Hamburg,
Germany